MW00449661

A Map of Future Ruins

Also by Lauren Markham

The Far Away Brothers:

Two Young Migrants and the Making of an American Life

A Map of Future Ruins

On Borders and Belonging

Lauren Markham

Riverhead Books
New York
2024

RIVERHEAD BOOKS
An imprint of Penguin Random House LLC
penguinrandomhouse.com

LIBRARY OF CONGRESS CATALOGING-IN-PUBLICATION DATA
Names: Markham, Lauren, author.
Title: A map of future ruins : on borders and belonging / Lauren Markham.
Description: First hardcover. | New York : Riverhead Books, [2024] |
Includes bibliographical references.
Identifiers: LCCN 2023027822 (print) | LCCN 2023027823 (ebook) |
ISBN 9780593545577 (hardcover) | ISBN 9780593545591 (ebook)
Subjects: LCSH: Greece—Emigration and immigration—History. |
Refugees—Greece—Social conditions. | Belonging (Social psychology)—Greece. |
Refugee camps—Greece. | Greece—Social conditions.
Classification: LCC JV8111 .M37 2024 (print) |
LCC JV8111 (ebook) | DDC 325.2109495—dc23/eng/20230706
LC record available at https://lccn.loc.gov/2023027822
LC ebook record available at https://lccn.loc.gov/2023027823

Printed in the United States of America
1st Printing

Book design by Cassandra Garruzzo Mueller

Some names and identifying characteristics have been changed
to protect the privacy of the individuals involved.

For my father, John Markham, the storyteller

A Map of Future Ruins

PART I

Present

1.

By September 2020, the rumors had begun. Something big was about to happen in Moria. People had had enough. Soon, some whispered, the refugee camp on the Greek island of Lesbos would be burned to the ground.

Moria was built in 2013, then expanded in 2015 as more and more refugee boats landed on Greece's shores. The camp was only ever meant to house 3,500 people at any given time, and only temporarily, but now, at the height of the global pandemic, some 11,000 people were crammed into Moria. "Welcome to hell!" old-timers would shout to the newly arrived, still waterlogged from the journey across the Aegean, as they registered at the main office and were told to find a place to sleep up in the hills beneath the olive trees. Stuck in limbo now, they jockeyed for position in the meal lines, at the filthy wash facilities and toilets, in the asylum queue.

Life in the camp was a prolonged purgatory, and it was easy to lose hope. A person's asylum process could take years—an interminable wait. People fell sick living among the refuse and excrement, the scampering rats. Fights broke out most nights. The place vibrated with the feeling of too many people in too-close quarters, as though something, at any moment, could blow. Every now and then, a Moria resident would threaten to set this hell on fire.

And this time, just as the rumors foretold, the camp went up in flames. Late on the night of September 8, a fire sparked in Zone 6, part of the informal camp that girded the official, walled camp like a boomerang, where everyone but those deemed most vulnerable lived. It was late enough when the fire began that most residents were already in their tents sleeping. The fire started out small, just a few tents. But it soon spread to the neighboring "Safe Zone," which housed the camp's minors, and within an hour much of the central camp was ablaze. The flames leaped easily between the makeshift shelters, which stood too closely packed in the olive groves, with barely room to walk among them. Curiously, other fires soon broke out in other areas of the camp—acres away from the first. As the fires caught hold, they sounded like dry, crackling rain. A good portion of Moria was on fire.

The flames made easy work of the plastic tarps, wooden lean-tos, and heaps of blankets and clothes, exposing the frames of the tents and structures—just bright, naked skeletons now, skinless and incandescent. The olive trees, too, caught fire, lifting the blaze higher into the smoke-choked sky.

As the fire sizzled and seethed with no sign of slowing, the people of Moria camp hurried to evacuate. The week before, the camp registered its first case of COVID-19, leading authorities to impose a camp-wide quarantine. As the flames tore through the camp, those who were locked up and slated for deportation had to break through the walls of their confinements to escape. People grabbed what they could—their phones, their chargers, their documents, their children—bundled their belongings into unwieldy piles, pulled masks or scarves over their faces, and ran. But in some places the fire had begun to form walls, hemming the residents in. Embers fell like hot snow and were pressed forward by the wind, catching hold of shirts and headscarves, trees and brittle grasses.

The small tents and IsoBoxes, miniature trailer-like structures that were among the better places to live in Moria, burst into flame, and frenzied rats skittered from the heat. In other places, the smoke obscured the pathways and rose higher into the night sky, which glowed a dazzling orange now. From the main road, practically all a person could see of the camp were silhouettes of the looping razor wire meant to keep the refugees in.

Within three hours of the initial sparks, the fire had begun to sound like a great, surging wave. It was visible from all sides of the camp, and all around the island, too; it lit up the night. The surrounding streets filled with people heading toward the safety of the capital city of Mytilene, some ten kilometers away in one direction, or the small town of Moria, for which the camp was named, in the other.

The growing far-right groups on the island quickly got word of the fire. They blocked the road to Moria town, where residents had gotten fed up with the refugees after they stole the villagers' goats (to have food to eat) and cut down their olive trees (to keep themselves warm in winter). In the other direction, police blockaded the road to Mytilene. This left thousands of refugees marooned on an empty stretch of road with no reliable food or water or medical care or bathrooms, let alone COVID safety measures. They'd stay there like this for days.

By the following morning, much of the camp had been turned to char and ash, the olive groves a smoldering copse of black harpoons. The wind—it happened to be particularly windy those days—carried the lingering embers, and more fires began. Those who had managed to stay now set off on the run. Every so often, someone would stop to record the fire with their phone—just standing there, swatting the embers away and taking it all in through their miniature screen. It was spectacular and terrifying, watching Moria be eaten alive.

Who started the fires? Theories abounded. The refugees lit the fires, some claimed, desperate to destroy their prison. The Afghans did it, some Arabs and Africans said. The Arabs did it, some Afghans declared. The fascists did it, others believed (they'd burned down a reception center on the island's north side a few years before) to rid the island of the refugees for good. Maybe it was the right-wing government, people on the left suggested. They, like the far-right factions, wanted the camp gone—wanted the rest of Greece, and the rest of Europe, to share in the work of housing the people who were continuing to flee metaphoric fires in their own homelands, and who were certain to keep crossing the Aegean, Europe-bound. A few even posited that one of the NGOs had started the fire, as a bid either to close the camp or to get more money, depending on whom you asked. Or perhaps the fire was merely an accident; by then, more than two hundred fires had erupted in the camp during the seven years since it had opened. But none of these claims was backed up by any concrete evidence.

And yet the government built a quick case. Just two days after the fire was extinguished, the minister of immigration announced that the authorities had found the perpetrators. That afternoon, six young Afghans were arrested.

Who knows how the fires really started. But now that the camp was finally gone, someone had to pay, and it seemed these six kids would do.

I'd begun traveling regularly to Greece in 2019, a year before the Moria fire. I went each time in pursuit of fact—to report on the refugee crisis and to research my family's history—but in the process I often found myself slipping into the territory of mythmaking, as if via a hole in the ground. This was, perhaps, predictable. For what is travel—and for that matter, what was my family's migration story, or even my choice to become a journalist—if not the pursuit of some mythic idea?

By the time I visited Greece, I'd heard much about Moria, a place that had amassed its own mythology, described so often as a kind of underworld. I planned to travel to Lesbos, where I'd visit the camp as a reporter. But first I'd spend some time on the mainland tourist trail with my husband, Ben, and visit the island where my ancestors once lived.

We set out into Athens early one morning with the hope of getting lost, but we were instantly sucked into the city's feverish tourist din. It was hard to escape. Within just a few blocks of our hotel, we'd found ourselves accidentally at the gates of the Acropolis, unwittingly tourists at the most obvious stop there was and among the very first in line. "In these classical lands," wrote French author Théophile Gautier in 1877, "the past is so alive that it leaves hardly any space for the present to survive." We had had no intention of exploring the ruins that morning, but we'd arrived before the demands of the crowds and the sun, so we decided to forgo aimlessness for the time being and pay our way inside.

We ascended the hill slowly, surveying the ancient, sun-bleached city as feral cats slinked through the shade and napped upon the rock. A less-traveled path—one generally closed to the public—wound us along the Acropolis's eastern edge, where a spring fell from the limestone in small droplets and bloodred poppies bloomed. Here the women of Athens once sought fertility blessings within the shallow caves. At the top of the hill stood the Parthenon, clanging with reconstruction, and from up there we could see all of Athens and far beyond. In this storied place, it was tempting to succumb to grand metaphors—to imagine myself situated at both the beginning and the end of something. By nine in the morning there were hundreds of us up on that hill, grasping at meaning.

From the Parthenon we followed our instincts away from the hordes of visitors and into the whitewashed neighborhood of Anafiotika, where rounded, ancient-looking houses crowded the hillside like honeycomb. Though a tourist trap in its own right, Anafiotika seemed miraculously empty, a hushed world of slender passages where, from time to time, a view would reveal the city below: the rushing snarl of Monastiraki, its cramped stalls and waiting taxis. But up there it was quiet and tranquil, difficult to discern public roadway from the entry to someone's home. We were finally unmapped, happy and in awe within the maze, having broken through the city's outermost husk and into a blissful disorientation in which we barely felt the need to speak.

After some minutes we rounded a bend where the hillside path opened to sky. There before us was an older gentleman seated on a low stool outside what we took to be his front door.

"Shh, shh!" the man hissed as we approached, waving a hand to demand our silence, though we hadn't been speaking. He was a sturdy block of a man who wore a brimmed cap from under which patches of white hair caught the light. At his feet sat a small wooden stringed instrument and an empty espresso cup, but his gaze was fixed on a blooming oleander that spilled over the pathway like a bridal arch. "Sit," he ordered, and we obliged, settling onto one of the stone steps in the oleander's shadow. A bird flitted through the dapple and the man grunted with delight, lifted his bouzouki, and began strumming, singing in Greek toward the trees.

"I speak bird," he announced over his forlorn song. We sat still and listened for a while. Then, as if he sensed we were about to take our leave, he spoke again.

"My name is Demetrios," he said, still strumming, motioning for us to stay a bit longer. "I speak bird because every day one thousand people are coming to Greece. One thousand! Syria, Afghanistan, Pakistan, Africa." We hadn't been in Greece twelve hours yet, but here it was already, talk of the refugees and what they were doing to the country's future. Demetrios insisted that it was just a matter of time before there would be no Greeks anymore. If he didn't speak bird, couldn't we see, soon there would be no one else to talk to.

"You know, a big mafia runs this country," Demetrios went on. "They want us to believe everything is okay. But it's not okay!" He pulled a tattered wallet from his pocket. See how little money he had stored in its folds? A wallet like this had once cost just a few euros, and now went for nearly three times that amount. And the coffee he drank each day, he said, pointing to his empty cup: how could a person afford coffee at this price? He shook his head and resumed his music. Greece, his home—it was changing, he felt, falling apart, turning to ruin.

It is possible to narrate an idea to death, wringing meaning dry. Another such story: that I'm Greek. Though most of my living family members have never been to Greece, the story of our Greekness is central to our identity. Its significance is teleological: being Greek means something because it is important to us that it mean something. I had come to Greece, in part, because I was determined to break out of this insistent loop, to get to the bottom of things. Many white people in the United States are animated by a similar longing to claim a faraway homeland, even as they support, explicitly or tacitly, the exclusion of contemporary migrants—people making a journey parallel to those their own ancestors made generations ago. I knew that to understand these contradictory instincts would require looking backward into my own family story, and further still into stories humans have created to make sense of our existence: that is, into myth.

Greece is a fraught place to claim as a personal origin story because it is also imagined as the origin of the entire so-called West: the birthplace of democracy, the dawn of Europe. For centuries, Europeans have been traveling to Greece to chart a backward lineage—not of their own families, as I was doing, but of civilization itself. "We hereby trace, as it were, our origin," writes Pierre-Augustin Guys in the preface to *A Sentimental Journey Through Greece*, in the 1700s, "at least, we may say, the source of our manners, and the fountain of our knowledge." Today, this origin story is further co-opted by white supremacist groups to claim genetic and cultural superiority.

Now Greece, this mythic personal and civilizational touchstone, had become a destination for so many people fleeing far more dire circumstances than had driven my own family from it a century before. Once in Greece, these refugees faced continued persecution and torment, for here, as in the United States and all over the world, migration was increasingly being cast as a crime—one to be fought and prevented, one for people to be punished for, it seemed, at all costs. All the while Greece itself, a place people visit for its ancient myths and its ruins, was forging troubling new mythologies and teetering, when viewed through a certain lens, toward ruin: its flailing economy, fires raging on land, a sea perilously overfished, a neo-Nazi party having risen prominently in the wings. I was struck by the way history folds upon itself, the way a single place can have been the setting for such a range of seismic human experience.

So there was the Greece of my family's stories and imaginations, the Greece of ancient civilization, the Greece of embattled borders and disappearing Greeks, the democratic and decent Greece dreamed about by refugees as they plotted their journeys across the seas, the Greece of the gods, the Greece of a ravaged economy forsaken by the rest of Europe, the Greece of the recent Nazi revival, the Greece that built the living nightmare of Moria camp. These competing versions of Greece each wrote their own mythologies that both nested within one another and bled into the next.

These were mirrors of the nesting mythologies that had taken hold back home in the States. My Greek family, for instance, like many white US American families, likes to narrate itself as an immigration success story wrought from sacrifice and hard work. This personalized myth is linked to a broader cultural fairy tale about the exceptional greatness of the United States, derived, in part, from the inheritance of classical ideas and ideals—which further lends itself to the mythologies that vilify newer immigrants, recasting the dynamic of flight into that of conquest, recasting the refugee as marauding invader. When steeped in this sort of dogma, a story tends to calcify, becoming statuary.

And here I was in Greece at last—my first visit but also some kind of wishful homecoming. We sat up on that shady hillside in Anafiotika for a while longer as Demetrios proffered his concert to the birds, a performance that was also, it seemed, for us. It occurred to me that he likely sat there all day long waiting for visitors to pass so he could sing his songs and tell tales of looming doom. What had felt at first like a spontaneous encounter was perhaps just another touristic sideshow—not so different from the stalls scattered about the city selling Acropolis statuettes, or the vendors hawking laurel crowns fashioned of flimsy wire. Demetrios could probably smell it on me, my desire to connect and belong.

Another bird dropped into our low cover. "I must talk bird," he repeated, "because soon there will be no Greek people anymore."

The future is forever on its way to upend the past. "Modern nostalgia," writes the theorist Svetlana Boym, "is a mourning for the impossibility of mythical return, for the loss of an enchanted world with clear borders and values." No matter where you go on earth you'll find someone pining for a homeland. And perhaps throughout time there has always been some old man on a hillside, strumming an instrument and sipping from a small cup, certain that because new people are coming and another layer is unfurling across history—that accumulation of moments, that sedimentary rock—his world is coming to an end.

A year after the Moria fire and two years after that first morning in Greece, I received a magazine assignment to write about the camp's destruction and the ensuing conviction of the six young men from Afghanistan. The Moria story was, to me, one of stunning injustice little told outside Europe, or even Greece—a story about far more than a fire and a rushed indictment; it revealed deeper truths about the poison of contemporary borders and practices of exclusion. Amid the complex contours of the project I was embroiled in, trying to understand the interplay among migration, myth, and memory in my family and in the wider world, it was a relief to receive such a clear-cut assignment. I expected my reporting to take the form of a relatively standard magazine piece: a linear story, one with a clear beginning, middle, and end.

But as it turned out, my investigation of the Moria case was inseparable from my larger project. As with the many versions of Greece, there were so many theories about how the fire had started, and why and by whom. Key facts were missing or withheld by those who knew them. How to tell a story with so many versions of the truth?

There was also the matter of deciding where and when such a story begins. Did it begin on the night of the fire—or perhaps when the rumors started, as I have chosen to begin this book? Did it begin with the COVID restrictions of March 2020 that locked people inside an effective tinderbox? In 2016, when the European Union brokered a deal with Türkiye that, among other things, warehoused refugees on the Aegean Islands? Or back in 2015, when the early boatloads of Syrians and then others washed ashore, sometimes ten thousand people in a single day? An argument could be made to start the story with the economic crisis of 2008, which turned Greece upside down and inside out. Or then again, in 1923, when Türkiye and Greece announced a population swap and thousands of Asia Minor Greeks were forced from their homes across the Aegean, many to Lesbos—landing on the very same rocks as today's refugees. Or during the great out-migration from Greece at the turn of the twentieth century, from which my own family traces origins. Maybe the place to begin was in 1797, when the first modern map of Greece was drawn, marring the landscape with borders. The more I researched, the further back my investigation took me.

There was the matter of how to write the Moria story, but in time I would also come to rethink why. In truth, after many years of reporting on borders, my belief in my role as a journalist, and in the efficacy of journalism more broadly, had begun to falter. What, in concrete terms, does writing such a story accomplish?

Ultimately the Moria story would end up not only connected to but central within my larger inquiry into the mechanics of belonging, exclusion, and whiteness in a heavily bordered world, the inquiry that had brought me to Greece in the first place—and central to the book that I would eventually write, this very book you hold in your hands, so different from how I first imagined it. For the story of the Moria fire and its aftermath, as I came to see it, was about the criminalization of contemporary migration, yes, but also about the valorization of times and migrations past.

In this sense and others, it was also a story about storytelling. The same grasping need to belong that had spawned those valorous myths of earlier migrations had created present-day immigration prisons like Moria. Such a camp could be read as a kind of narrative in and of itself: a place that froze time, that fixed the story of a person's life into a predetermined sequence and a limited set of outcomes, like a piece of hack reporting. Whoever set the fire—if indeed it had been deliberately set—must have been attempting to disrupt some perceived order of things, that is, to revise the story.

I had been drawn to writing about Greece because I was interested in the way the stories of catastrophe, displacement, and belonging were told: which stories get passed along, what gets passed off as true, and the consequences of all that goes missing along the way. How we tell our stories determines, individually and collectively, our ideologies, our policies, and our actions, and the way we construct our physical worlds. How people chose to read the Moria story was thus a barometer of their belief systems and of how they wanted the world to be. For I knew from the way my own family told our story of migration from Greece to the United States, and of our belonging to both places, that a story is never just a story. A story is also an oracle: it tells the future.

2.

Back in 2015 I'd seen the news—who hadn't?—of the boats washing ashore on Greek islands with their bedraggled charges, the onslaught of headlines: "Bodies of 11 Refugees, Most of Them Infants, Recovered off Greece. Cash-Strapped Greece Struggles Against Overwhelming Tide of Refugees." And then there was the photograph of the little red-shirted boy, facedown dead on the beach where the waves had left him. In the arms of the Turkish soldier, his limbs went slack in the way of a child merely sleeping. His name was Alan Kurdi. A refugee from Syria, he was only three years old when he drowned, Europe-bound. His death quickly became a symbol, his likeness reproduced ad infinitum in newspapers and humanitarian memes and works of public art. The symbol did its work in the international shallows: leaders vowed to intervene on behalf of refugees crossing the Mediterranean, and the world, me included, turned its head to pay attention for a spell. But people kept crossing, people kept dying, nothing much changed. And most of the people who had been paying attention moved on.

"Politicians said after the death of my family: never again!" Alan's father told the press. "Everyone allegedly wanted to do something after the photos that had so moved them. But what is happening now? The dying goes on, and nobody's doing anything." Mr. Kurdi also pleaded with would-be refugees not to cross the sea. It was just too dangerous, the odds of death too high. But people kept coming anyway, for, as the oft-quoted poem by Warsan Shire goes, "no one leaves home unless / home is the mouth of a shark."

Ali Sayed knew nothing of the crisis in Greece. He hadn't heard the news on the radio or seen it online or on TV—not even the image of the little boy facedown on the Turkish sand. Young as he was, Ali Sayed was well aware of the ongoing exodus of people from his country, but the only thing he knew of Greece—or Unan, as the place was called in Afghanistan—was those statues and buildings from the ancient world.

Ali attended school in Afghanistan for six years. When he was nine, he got a job repairing boots so he could help support his family. After the US invasion, one of his older brothers began working for the Marines as an interpreter. When US military sympathizers became targets in Afghanistan, his brother was offered protection from the US government: passage elsewhere. Ali's brother, along with his wife and two children, resettled in California—that mythic, far-off place that Ali knew from movies and songs. His brother opened a refrigerator-repair business in Sacramento and occasionally sent money home, but it wasn't enough to support the family.

Ali left school to work more hours. Even as a little boy he understood that the life he wanted, modest though it was—an education, a job, a home, a family safe from war—required leaving Afghanistan. People left, and left, and left.

"His story is the story of any boy from Afghanistan," his brother would tell me years later.

So when Ali was thirteen, he packed a bag and crossed the border into Iran. There, he figured, he could at least speak the language and thus would be more likely to find work. But millions of other Afghans hoped for the same. Between 3 and 4 million Afghans reside in Iran, of whom only about 780,000 are registered refugees. As in the United States, the undocumented are easily exploited in the workplace, or barred from getting jobs at all. Iran had economic and political challenges of its own, and no one seemed to want to give a thirteen-year-old Afghan kid a job, so after a year of trying, Ali moved on across the next border, into Türkiye.

He found that things were even more difficult for migrants in Türkiye, which hosts 4 million refugees, largely from Syria and Afghanistan, and whose government lambasts "the West" for not doing more to support them. Migrants travel through Türkiye en route to Europe, and many Afghans have fled to the country as a direct result of the United States' longest war. Vigilante violence against refugees in Turkish cities and towns is common, and Turkish authorities are quick to round up those without documentation and put them in removal centers, sometimes for days and sometimes for months, sometimes releasing them back out onto the Turkish streets and sometimes deporting them home.

In Türkiye, Ali continued to look for work and even tried to secure papers, only to learn that doing so would be nearly impossible. So he remained undocumented and did what he could to avoid the authorities. The first months, he scrounged the trash for scraps and asked around for a safe place to sleep. In spite of his best efforts, he wound up in prison several times. They'd keep him for a while, then let him go. Eventually he found employment at a carpet factory in a small town near Ankara, which allowed him food and a steady place to sleep, though not much else. He still wasn't making enough to send money home.

It was in Türkiye that he first heard about modern-day Greece—that country on the edge of Europe, that luminous, treacherous gateway. Because he was young, his Afghan coworkers at the rug factory told him, he'd get favorable treatment in Europe. Germany was the place to go, if he could get there. In Germany, people said, he would be given papers and food and housing and would even be able to go back to school. That way he could get a well-paid job that would allow him to live a forward-moving life and to send money back home to Afghanistan: the reasons he'd left in the first place.

To get to Germany he'd first have to cross the border into Europe, and to do that he'd have to cross the sea, which meant saving up 1,000 euros for a seat on a boat. He worked for months until he had the money, then traveled to Istanbul to meet the smugglers. He had just enough for a ticket for the cramped ride but not enough for a life jacket—that cost extra. He'd heard that the life jackets smugglers provided were fakes anyway; if you fell in the sea, they swamped with water, hauling you under more swiftly and decisively than if you wore nothing at all.

By this point Ali had also heard about the shipwrecks, all the people who'd been sucked into the deeps of the Aegean. Smugglers often crammed fifty, sixty, eighty people into a vessel meant to hold twenty at most. The men tended to sit on the outside, while the women and children sat in the boat's interior. Even when the boats made it, they often arrived barely floating after hours at sea. At least once, a boat reached shore and a mother stood up only to find that her baby had drowned or suffocated in her arms.

Making it across, Ali understood, was a gamble. But any direction he went would require a gamble, a risk. The smugglers ushered him to the coast, where the group crept through the brush until they reached their boat: a damaged inflatable the size of a large pickup. Ali couldn't believe how many of them were corralled onto that vessel. There were old people, tiny children, men and women, boys traveling alone just like him.

On board, the other passengers pressed against him from all sides and took turns reinflating the leaking pontoons. There was a forced intimacy in their shared passage, but at the same time these were all perfect strangers to him—he was just a sixteen-year-old floating across the map of the world, all on his own. What was there to do but pray?

The smugglers designated one of the group to steer the boat, then pushed the vessel away from shore. (Human smuggling rings in Türkiye don't risk the lives of their workers, or the valuable space in the boat, by sending any of them along on the passage to Greece. Instead, they force the refugees themselves to captain their way to safety.) They were on their own now. The group passed the night on the darkened waters, trying to keep their bearings. To scream or moan could summon the Turkish authorities; to shift too quickly in the boat could cause it to tip. When the darkness lifted to reveal morning, the passengers could see land in the distance—which land, exactly, they weren't sure. Soon, they spotted a boat headed their way. It was the Greek Coast Guard. The officials unloaded the passengers and brought them into port. Ali stepped off, stiff and wobbly-legged, onto land again. So this—this was Europe.

They were taken from the rocky coast to a transit camp, where they were registered as asylum seekers and given health screenings, a meal, and a place to sleep. When asked his age, Ali told them he was sixteen years old, but, he recalls, the official taking down his information didn't believe him.

"We Afghans look old," he would later explain. He'd lived a lot of life already, and he believed it showed on his face, though his lawyers would later comment on just how young he looked, how he was so obviously a minor, just a kid. The authorities insisted on listing him as an eighteen-year-old, which angered him, but what could he do? He was alive, which was the most important thing, and in Europe—on the long path to his future. Little did he know how crucial this bit of bureaucracy would prove to be.

From the transit station, Ali was taken to Moria. His first memory of the camp: the customary "Welcome to hell" shouted down from the hillsides in greeting as the bus passed through the front gates. It was part taunt, part joke, but, he found, Moria was indeed a kind of hell. Because he'd been registered as an adult rather than as an unaccompanied minor, he'd get no protective housing, no special food, no mental health services or regular school, no prioritized legal support for his asylum case. He was assigned a tent with three other men in the olive groves and given a meal card that allowed him to queue up every day for food. The first few nights, he could barely sleep or eat out of fear—of the crowds, of the fights and shouting, of what would befall him here. Had he made the right choice to come?

The conflicts in the camp were sometimes between rival gangs, sometimes between groups from different countries of origin, and sometimes simply between friends who had had too much to drink or too much of the confinement. Ali was also surprised to find that ethnic conflicts from home had followed him here. His family was Shia, from one of Afghanistan's minority groups. Many of his new neighbors were Hazara. Considered to be among the most persecuted peoples in the world, the Hazaras had once been widely enslaved. In the nineteenth century, a campaign of ethnic cleansing by a leader from the Sunni Pashtun majority killed more than half their population and displaced many others. In 1998, thousands of Hazaras were executed by the Taliban. The centuries-old tensions that persisted in Afghanistan surfaced in Moria, thousands of miles from home.

Though Ali and the other refugees were permitted to move around the island of Lesbos—to take the bus into town to buy groceries or have a coffee or meet with an immigration attorney or take a dip in the sea—the camp often felt like a prison. The island, the more Ali thought of it, was also a kind of prison. Surrounded by water, it was impossible to leave. Well, not impossible. Some paid to be smuggled onto large trucks that loaded onto the ships headed for the mainland, but such an escape was expensive, hard to manage, and dangerous, too.

He hoped he'd sort his papers and be off Lesbos soon. Ali liked to picture the streets of Athens and imagined walking free there, asylum card in his pocket and bound for Germany, eventually—bound for life. Often he called his brother in California to ask for help. Sometimes his brother sent money, but most times he didn't. He had a family of his own to support, his brother explained, and he was already supporting the rest of the siblings back in Afghanistan.

To pass the time, Ali volunteered in his zone's food line, helping to keep order and pass out boxed meals. If he had to be stuck here, at least he wanted to be of some use. Weeks passed, then months. Still no word on his asylum case. He avoided the fights, avoided getting sick, tried to stay sane and alive and to keep his hopes aloft.

But it wasn't easy. The conditions in the Aegean camps like Moria had drawn international criticism for years, and as they became more crowded, things only got worse. According to the international medical aid organization Médecins San Frontières, in 2019 there was only one shower for every 506 people living in Moria. In the camp on the nearby island of Samos, 300 people shared a single toilet. That year, as arrivals increased and transfers off the islands slowed, mental health referrals in the camps increased 40 percent from the previous year.

"If not urgently and adequately addressed," said Dunja Mijatović, the Council of Europe's commissioner for human rights, during a visit to Moria in the fall of 2019, around the time Ali arrived, "these abysmal conditions, combined with existing tensions, risk leading to further tragic events." Looking back, this statement reads like a prophecy.

When does a story begin? Ask people in Lesbos, as I would do again and again, to tell me the story of the Moria fire and they will, without fail, begin long before the first sparks incinerated the camp to mere memory of itself.

The vast majority of refugees who'd arrived since 2015, having fled war and persecution and environmental collapse, ended up on the island of Lesbos, and in Moria camp. Here, like Ali, they would only encounter further violence, injustice, and loss. "No more Moria!" had become a rallying cry of both the right and the left, in Greece and all across Europe. To the right, the slogan signified "No more refugees on our islands, in our lands." To the left, it meant "No more internment camps for people seeking refuge from war and persecution," which, after all, was their right under domestic and international law. By the time it burned down, nearly everyone had reason to want Moria gone.

That Moria existed at all was a function of the EU law that compelled the member state in which a refugee first arrived to handle that person's asylum claim—most often countries on the periphery—to host arriving refugees until their asylum claims were decided, and of Greece's decision to warehouse the refugees in key "hotspot" islands, like Lesbos, in the Aegean.

In 2019, the situation for asylum seekers in Greece had taken a further turn when a center-right party swept local and national elections, running, in part, on the rhetoric of border security. After the new government assumed power that July, refugee transfers off the Aegean Islands began to slow. At the same time, more and more refugees were arriving; that year, nearly 60,000 people made it across the Aegean to Greece, compared with just 32,000 the year before.

"We are going to take measures to protect our borders, and we are going to be much stricter, much faster in applying them," Greece's minister of citizen protection told a Greek newspaper as the boats hurried across the sea.

But by September, so many people were arriving each week that the Hellenic Coast Guard made urgent appeals to EU border forces for assistance. Meanwhile, the new Greek government passed legislation severely limiting NGOs' activities, including search-and-rescue operations at sea. In some estimations, this made it illegal to assist with a shipwreck in Greek waters, in defiance of international maritime law, which requires all vessels to come to the aid of any boat in distress. Under the new regime, it was now up to the Coast Guard alone to patrol for sinking boats—and there was no one to monitor what the Coast Guard was really up to, out at sea. By January 2020, a few months after Ali arrived, some twenty thousand people were living in Moria—more than six times the number it was designed to house. The Ministry of Migration and Asylum announced a plan for the island: they would build a new camp and shutter the three existing camps—Moria; a smaller, government-run camp called Kara Tepe; and an unofficial camp run by local and international volunteers with an anarchist bent, known as Pikpa. The new facility would be built in the middle of the island, in a remote place called Vastria. It would be constructed deep in the forest, walled off and hidden from view.

Hardly anyone was happy with this solution, either. The left-wingers believed the new camp, built on the US detention center model, was a fundamental violation of human rights and would limit refugees' ability to access services, including legal assistance, education, and mental health support. To the right-wingers, the construction of a new camp signaled that there was no end in sight to refugees' living on Lesbos. Protests from both factions erupted on the island in January and February.

International developments further complicated matters on Lesbos. On February 29, Turkish president Recep Tayyip Erdoğan announced that his government would no longer be patrolling the borders between Türkiye and Europe to keep refugees from crossing, as they had done since 2016 when the so-called EU–Turkey deal was signed. After Erdoğan's announcement, both land and sea borders were, in the eyes of EU policymakers, doors left ajar; the refugees no longer had to evade Turkish authorities to make it to the European Union. In response, the EU sent military assistance to ramp up border patrols, and Greece began to force arrivals back to Türkiye or summarily detain them once they landed on shore.

During this time, Ali sat in Moria, still waiting for news of his asylum interview. He waited and waited. When he was finally assigned a date, he rejoiced, but the date was pushed back, and then pushed back again. This was common. It could take years for an asylum application to progress through the system. All of Ali's hopes hung on this interview: a chance to plead his case—and thus a chance to stay in Europe.

After Erdoğan's announcement, the Greek authorities on Lesbos began to lock up all newly arrived refugees behind metal fences at the Mytilene port. "They were kept there like criminals," Amelia Cooper of Legal Centre Lesvos, a nonprofit providing direct services to refugees, recalled to me. She and her colleagues would go down to the port each day to monitor human rights abuses and take testimonies from the prisoners.

One day, Amelia told me, a fifteen-year-old boy from Syria pleaded to her through the chain-link fence: "Tell Mama Merkel," he said to her in Arabic. "Tell Mama Merkel what is happening to us here." He was certain she'd be shocked at the abuses he and his fellow refugees were suffering. After such a long journey, he had to believe something better and more humane awaited him than what he'd left behind. Surely, if German chancellor Angela Merkel knew, she would set them free.

"Oh," Amelia thought as she stood at the fence, "this poor boy. He has no idea. He's going to be crushed." It is a terrible thing when myths crumble before one's very eyes.

3.

It has always been the prime function of mythology and rite," wrote Joseph Campbell, "to supply the symbols that carry the human spirit forward, in counteraction to those other constant human fantasies that tend to tie it back." In this sense, myths are the formative tales that reflect who we are and that offer guidance for how to live—both practically upon a landscape and also morally. But another meaning of the word *myth* is "invention" or "deception." Sometimes such deceptions are forged willfully, spun by those in power or in pursuit of it—as seems easier and easier to do in the age of the nation-state, especially with the advent of viral media. In other cases, these myths seem to bloom from an imbalance in the human ecosystem at a given moment, a state of collective fear or loss, for instance, that creates a wish for something other than the present reality to be true. In all cases, these sorts of myths can be read as ferocious dirges that, rather than "carry the human spirit forward," propel a populace back toward an imagined time of national and racial purity. My work as a journalist, I felt, was to face these myths head-on.

Central to today's pernicious political mythologies is the myth of Western identity itself. White-dominated societies continue to look to the so-called ancient world as an ideological origin story, mapping ancient Greece and Rome not just at the center of that world but as the entirety of it. "From the late middle ages until now," writes the scholar Kwame Anthony Appiah, "people have thought of the best in the culture of Greece and Rome as a civilisational inheritance, passed on like a precious golden nugget."

What is "the West," really, anyway? A story fashioned in reverse to explain the present: a myth. It wasn't until the 1890s—the height of European empire and conquest—that the idea and terminology of "the West" really emerged. And as Appiah points out, it wasn't until the Cold War that the idea of "Western culture" arose. "In the chill of battle," he argues, "we forged a grand narrative about Athenian democracy, the Magna Carta, Copernican revolution, and so on." In this mythic imagining, the West is, as Appiah puts it, "individualistic and democratic and liberty-minded and tolerant and progressive and rational and scientific. Never mind that pre-modern Europe was none of these things, and that until the past century democracy was the exception in Europe."

Even the notion of European identity is a myth—in the sense of the word that connotes pure invention. Appiah points out that in the *Histories*, a discursive account of the centuries of conflicts between Greeks and their neighbors, written in the fifth century BCE, Herodotus never uses the term "European" to describe a distinct group. "For a millennium after his day," Appiah writes, "no one else spoke of Europeans as a people, either." The Europeans, he contends, began to think of themselves as such only with the rise of Christianity across the continent, and only as an identity in opposition to that of the Muslims to their south and east.

The Renaissance played its part. In the fourteenth century, as the bubonic plague surged in what we now call Europe, the world seemed to be coming to an end. The Italian poet Petrarch was overcome with grief and horror at what he saw all around him: the disfigurement of human bodies, the bodies piling up in the streets, the streets emptying of living people. "On all sides is sorrow," he wrote to his brother, "everywhere is fear." Italian thinkers began to reconsider the order of things, "consciously turning their backs on the medieval notion of the universe," according to the notes for an exhibition at Frankfurt's Liebieghaus Sculpture Collection. In search of guidance, they looked to the past: the Greek and Roman empires. "They took Classical Antiquity as their cue for a new system of values and image of man," the exhibition explains. To move forward, they looked back in time.

Petrarch and his contemporaries scoured the continent's remote libraries to recover lost manuscripts from ancient Greece and Rome. "Let them search through Etruria and empty out the closets of holy orders and other studious persons," he wrote to friends, "in case anything should emerge suited to soothe or either stimulate my thirst." The thirst was for solid guidance in an unstable time: ideas about how to govern, how to make art, how to live. The classical era seemed like it could provide such a touchstone—a touchstone to which civilization must return. After a Greek magistrate sent him a Homeric text in the original Greek, Petrarch, who considered Homer "the wellspring and origin of all literary creation," wrote a fawning letter of thanks for the work "not translated in some foreign speech brewed from a violent cauldron, but pure and uncorrupted from the fountain of Greek eloquence itself, just as it first flowed from [Homer's] divine intellect."

These recovered manuscripts helped launch a new era of thought that Petrarch himself christened "the Renaissance"—distinct from the "dark ages" that had followed the fall of the Roman Empire. The humanists, as Renaissance scholars became known (fathers of what we now think of as "the humanities"), were interdisciplinary in their studies, just as the ancients had been, but they tended to be concerned especially with the study of power and morality, stemming in part from the virtue ethics of Aristotle. Morality was not to be confined to the realm of religion; it was also central to daily life and to politics, and it was morality, not merely birthright or divine mandate, that should determine who might hold power. "For the humanists," as the scholar James Hankins explains, "what gives rulers legitimacy are personal qualities of character and intellect that win trust and obedience from the ruled."

The collapse of the Byzantine Empire to the Ottomans in the mid-fifteenth century only deepened the Renaissance preoccupation with ancient Greece. Whereas the Western Roman Empire had succumbed to invaders in the fifth century CE, the Eastern Roman Empire, which included the Greek city-states—"Hellas"—largely survived for over a millennium in what we now know as the Byzantine Empire. When its capital, Constantinople, fell to the Ottomans in 1453, scads of scholars fled the city to Italy and other parts of western Europe, bringing with them their own preoccupation with classical Greek texts, which had experienced a revival in the East and were central to the intellectual tradition in which these scholars had been formed. Some of these Greek refugees took up posts in Italian universities, where they taught Greek, translated ancient Greek texts, and fomented classical thought—the ideas they'd brought with them, which they were delighted to discover had also been resuscitated in their new homes.

Then, in 1489, Italians unearthed an ancient Roman sculpture of Apollo. The Apollo Belvedere, as the statue came to be known, gleamed white and noble, nude but for a cape draped from the neck of the god. The arms were outstretched, having just released an arrow from his quiver, perhaps to slay the python guarding the cleft at Delphi. "From far and wide," recount the Liebieghaus exhibition notes, "scholars and artists flocked to the Apollo Belvedere to study and copy it. They extolled the skillful representation, noting that the white marble emphasizes the form of the body and creates a charming play of light and shadow."

By then, more than a century after Petrarch's death, the plague had all but disappeared from Europe, and the Renaissance was in full bloom. Architects were constructing new buildings with Doric and Ionic columns to resemble the buildings of ancient Greece and Rome, and there was a renewed focus on reason, science, order, and symmetry in intellectual and artistic life. During the so-called dark ages, the fine arts in northern Europe had largely depicted religious subjects, but now historical and mythical iconography were fair game. Artists began painting in the classical style and sculpting with the celebrated formal realism of the classical period, emphasizing the use of bare materials—marble, stone, and bronze—as they understood the ancients to have done. Soon, the Frankfurt exhibition explained, painting was deemed largely superficial as an art form, its "depth merely the result of optical trickery." The use of color was just a distraction. Sculpture: that was real art. From the Renaissance came the tendency, as Margaret Talbot writes in "The Myth of Whiteness in Classical Sculpture," to "equate whiteness with beauty, taste, and classical ideals, and to see color as alien, sensual, and garish."

The Renaissance thinkers believed they were originalists, reviving the past clean and uncorrupted. But in turning to the classical era as a sourcebook for their own art and ideas, they were simultaneously excavating the past and writing a new, selective version of history into being, shaped not only by the omissions and obscurities of time but by their own biases and desires. As the scholar Craig Kallendorf puts it, "Each postclassical age recreates the classical past as part of its effort to see back into it."

The unearthed classical sculptures, for instance, weren't originally displayed as they are today—as just sculpted material void of pigment. We now know they had been painted lavishly, in bold colors that had almost entirely faded and been worn away by the elements as the centuries went by. The notion of an artistic tradition founded on bare white stone that the Renaissance artists embraced was all a misunderstanding of the past—as tangled and entrenched as the notion of ancient Greece as the birthplace of "the West."

The myth of Greece as civilizational origin story is what, along with its beaches, still draws hordes of tourists to the country each year, clambering up the Acropolis to behold what they've been told is an epicenter of history. From nearly everywhere in central Athens you can see the Parthenon perched upon its hilltop, illuminated against the night sky—a constant reminder of the past and of Western civilization's original glory. "Arching, leaning, straining, swelling, breathing," notes the writer Daniel Mendelsohn in *The New Yorker*, "the overall effect of the Parthenon's architectural subtleties is to give the building a special and slightly unsettling quality of being somehow alive." In 2022, some sixteen thousand visitors walked through the Acropolis turnstiles every single day, often braving, as I did that first morning in Greece and several times after, the heat and crowds in order to ascend that fabled peak and seek some sort of transmission from the past.

One day, in search of refuge from Athens's infernal swelter, Ben and I ducked into the Acropolis Museum at the base of the hill. Built in 2009 of gleaming glass and steel, it was constructed around and atop the ruins as though in a waltz with the past. We approached along a sheet of thick glass that let us peer down into the excavation of the city's ancient remains. A fountain down there was filled with modern coins—wishes for the future cast into a vessel from long ago.

Inside the museum it was cool and spare—the weathered traces of the ancient city now mounted in the echoing, window-lit galleries. We walked among the displays, aware that we were observing not only works of art and architecture but the handiwork of time and of human curation.

The museum chronicled the evolution of the Parthenon over many hundreds of years. It made clear that there was in fact no single definitive "Parthenon," but rather a structure that was continuously remodeled as changing trends and needs dictated the addition of new elements in new styles, and as eras of destruction required that it be rebuilt and reconceived. Though it is now most often described as a temple erected under the politician Pericles in the first century BCE to honor the city's patron goddess, Athena, since the first of its stones was laid the Parthenon has also served as a church, a mosque, an arms repository—and perhaps even as a temple commemorating human sacrifice.

"Just about everyone who has ever struggled up the slippery marble steps of the Acropolis and gazed at this astonishing building seems to have wanted to lay claim to it," Mendelsohn reflects. But what does the Parthenon really stand for? Up on that hillside, or from the living city below, it felt as if the place could mean whatever a person wanted it to mean.

In 1975, the Greek government undertook a massive restoration of the Parthenon—the largest, most ambitious restoration in modern history, one intended to situate Greece at the center of the historical pilgrimage map of Europe yet again. The archaeological team, with the backing of the government, decided to fashion the ruins according to its preferred idea of the ancients, never mind all that the building had been and served as since. "Relatively few scholars or archeologists since 1832, when Greece won its independence from the Turks, have questioned that the correct way to 'restore' the Acropolis was to strip away all evidence of those subsequent incarnations—to return it to the Golden Age of Pericles," writes Mendelsohn. The restoration of the Parthenon as we see it today was a project, then, of nation building—a storytelling project, the construction of a myth.

The historian Roderick Beaton suggests that "so used are we, today, to thinking of 'modern Greece' as an offshoot of ancient Greece, it can be hard to realize that for many of the centuries separating classical antiquity from ourselves no such sense of affinity existed among Greek speakers." But after Greece won independence in 1832, politicians launched a nationalist revival, claiming a direct, unmitigated lineage from the ancients, just as the rest of Europe was doing. Greeks began to christen their children with the names of the ancients: Penelope, Calliope, Despina, Socrates. Such were the names of my own family members who set sail from Greece to the USA and who were born soon after arriving, living artifacts of this resurrection who were, simultaneously, part of a distinct new national era: that of the great Greek diaspora.

The Acropolis Museum, which drew nearly fifteen million visitors during its first ten years, was constructed as part of this nation-building continuum. The museum told many stories, but chief among them was that of theft and loot. In the early 1800s, when Greece was still under Ottoman rule, Lord Elgin, a British diplomat to Constantinople, stripped the Parthenon of sculptures and shipped them home. (The ship ran aground on its way back to Britain, and it took three years to excavate Elgin's loot from the bottom of the Mediterranean Sea.) He would eventually sell them to the British Museum. Known variably as the Parthenon Marbles or the Elgin Marbles, depending on to whom one believes they belong, the sculptures are still on display at the British Museum today. For in spite of Greece's best efforts, the British refuse their return, having in 1963 deemed it illegal to dispose of any of the museum's holdings and insisting, in the neocolonial attitude that still characterizes northern Europe's relationship to Greece, that the marbles were acquired under legal contract with the Ottomans, are in fact "shared heritage" of all of Europe, and enjoy a far wider audience and better care in the custody of the Brits than they would with the Greeks.

There, outside the Acropolis Museum's immense windows, stood the resurrected Parthenon itself: site of plunder, screen of projection. While its design, as Mendelsohn points out, is now considered the epitome of classical style—with its triangular pediments, its fluted Doric columns, the sculpted frieze that wraps around the entire building—at the time of its construction (in other words, its renovation) it was a marvel of the new: "typical of nothing at all, an anomaly in terms of material, size, and design."

Although the museum itself was muted and monochrome, it also corrected the narrative with regard to color. The day we visited, a digital exhibition traced contemporary art historians' attempts to piece together what classical sculptures really looked like in their original full color. We scrolled through the images on a large screen. The reconstructed polychromatic images—a winged, sphinxlike creature with the pencil-thin eyebrows of a nineties pop star, for instance, and a Trojan prince with an impish smile and psychedelic-patterned leggings of the sort I might impulse-buy at Target—felt fanciful, even shocking, as if from a storybook for children. I admit to preferring the old versions, the ones I was used to—the stories, in effect, that I'd grown comfortable living within.

Established narratives can be difficult to revise. For centuries, Talbot explains, art historians and archaeologists routinely found flecks of paint on the classical marble and stone they were unearthing. But instead of recognizing these traces as clues, they scrubbed the sculptures clean of them. "This ardor for whiteness was so intense," she writes, "that the evidence didn't stand a chance."

In the mid-eighteenth century, the Dutch anatomist Pieter Camper set out to determine the mathematical formula for ideal beauty, using the Apollo Belvedere as his gold standard. He spent years sawing apart skulls and traveling the world to take measurements of the facial features of people throughout northern and southern Europe, Africa, and the Middle East. He determined that the angles of the average European face most closely resembled the ideal beauty sculpted by the ancient Greeks, and that the angles of most African faces indicated both lesser beauty and lesser intelligence. He passed off this racial ranking as science, helping lay the groundwork for phrenology—the pseudoscience that would become an ideological cornerstone of the Third Reich.

Nazi iconography also drew from the classical tradition. Adolf Hitler was particularly taken with the Discobolus, a seminal sculpture of a rippling young athlete bending forward, one foot behind the other, on the verge of casting a discus. He eventually managed to purchase a replica of it in 1938 for the price of 5 million lire. To Hitler it represented the ideal human form, possessing beauty, strength, valor—and whiteness.

Nothing in the historical record suggests that ancient Greece itself had a collective identity of whiteness—or that the notion of whiteness had even arisen by that point at all. In fact, the ancient world was largely multiethnic, a crossroads of many lands and peoples. In revisiting the long-erased colors of the classical world, archaeologists and art historians have determined that the skin tones painted onto marble reflected a wide range of colors and ethnicities, few of them very light-skinned. In this context, writes the historian and artist Nell Irvin Painter, skin color wasn't a social signifier. "What mattered was where they lived; were their lands damp or dry; were they virile or prone to impotence, hard or soft; could they be seduced by the luxuries of civilized society or were they warriors through and through? What were their habits of life?"

Even so, classical iconography continues to be a touchstone of white supremacy today, building off the myth that ancient Greece is the taproot of so-called Western culture (a euphemism for white culture) and that there is such a thing as "Western identity" to begin with—one that must be resuscitated if "white" societies are to return to their former glory. The growing movement Identity Evropa, for instance, rebranded as the American Identity Movement until it was disbanded in 2020, littered US college campuses with posters of classical-style sculptures overlaid with white supremacist slogans. There was the statue of David (*Let's Become Great Again*), or one of Hercules (*Protect Your Heritage*), or the neoclassical head of Julius Caesar (*Serve Your People*). One poster, observes the art critic Ben Davis on Artnet, portrays a sculpture of a child, innocent eyes upturned, with the quotation "Our Destiny Is Ours." But the child was not, in fact, a classical or even neoclassical sculpture, Davis found. "The best guess is that it is invoked by Identity Evropa, not because of what it actually represents, but because it just *looks* evocative of the right thing." In order to claim dominance, white supremacists must concoct an origin story and cling so tightly to it that nothing—not what is right, not what is true—can loosen that grip.

In 2019, the Trump administration leaked a draft executive order titled "Make Federal Buildings Beautiful Again" prior to its official announcement. The order decreed that classical architecture would be the "preferred and default style" for any new construction of federal buildings in DC.

As with the Parthenon, the design of government structures is an exercise in nationalism, which is in and of itself an identity project: an attempt to simultaneously harness a lineage and cement a future story. The original guiding principles for the design of US federal buildings, written in 1962 by Daniel Patrick Moynihan, asserted that these buildings "must provide visual testimony to the dignity, enterprise, vigor, and stability of the American government." Already, many US buildings harked back to classicism. "Like all Greeks," remarked Greek prime minister Kyriakos Mitsotakis when addressing Congress in 2022, "every time I come to Washington I feel as if I'm coming home, because everything I see around me, the architecture, the art, the ideas carved into marble throughout the city, is so familiar."

Moynihan's guidelines strictly eschewed the imposition of an official style or even any form of "excessive uniformity," even going as far as to say that the government ought to be willing to spend additional funds to avoid it. But Trump and his people wanted columns, gleaming marble, triumphal arches, references to the Parthenon before it turned to ruin, before it was overrun by languorous cats, before the empire fell. They sought to evoke an imaginary time when civilization was both great and white.

These are the sorts of mythologies that proliferate today and threaten to steer our future. What Svetlana Boym calls "restorative nostalgia" is a project of reincarnating a nonexistent past when things were better, people and ideas more pure. This form of nostalgia is a fundamentally nationalist project, an "anti-modern myth-making of history," as she calls it, that relies on nationalist symbols, mythologies, and conspiracy theories. But restorative nostalgics don't see themselves as mythmakers; they "believe that their project is about truth."

In the fifth century BCE, the Persians made their way to Athens, burning and pillaging everything en route. Nearly all of Athens had been evacuated in anticipation of warfare. By the time the Persians reached the city it was deserted, save for a few elders who had barricaded themselves inside the buildings. The elders threw rocks at the invaders, who in turn set the hillside aflame with burning arrows, smashed the stone buildings, and burned the wood structures to the ground. A sacred olive tree blessed by Athena caught fire, too. "The elaborate Acropolis," a placard in the Acropolis Museum explained, "was turned into a vast ruin."

Upon their return, the Athenians vowed not to rebuild right away but, for a while at least, to "leave the ruins as they were in order to remind succeeding generations of the traumatic events endured by the city and its sanctuary." When the Parthenon was finally rebuilt, it was given yet another new look. The builders made a point of inscribing the structure with narrative: carving images of the city's past greatness into its upper walls—stories of the conquests of Greek mortals and gods (centuries later, many of these friezes would be stolen by Lord Elgin). Thus the Parthenon was revived from ruin as both a monument to war and a textbook of fragmented history.

The new Parthenon ensured that generations of Athenians would not forget the time when their city was pillaged and their forebears became refugees. During the war, most men had sent their wives and children to shelter in a city in the Peloponnese called Troezen. "The Troezens welcomed the Athenians," I read on a small museum placard, "offered them some money to get by, allowed their children to freely eat the fruit of the trees and took measures to ensure that teachers were available to educate their children." The exiles were taken care of until they could safely go back home.

Offering the sort of refuge the Troezens provided the Athenians is an ancient practice—one that appears in Hebrew, Greek, Roman, and Islamic texts from thousands of years ago. In ancient Greece, an asylum seeker could enter a foreign city, find his way to a designated house of refuge—typically a temple or sanctuary—and twist an olive branch around his arm to signal his need for protection. The Greeks once largely believed a moral function of the state was to provide haven for those whose lives were at risk elsewhere, but they also offered the opportunity to seek asylum because politicians feared the wrath both of the demos and of the gods if they did not.

"Refuge, sanctuary, truce, political pardon—these were elemental concepts woven into the fabric of the earliest democracies," writes the journalist John Washington. In fact, he says, the word *asylum* itself is derived from the Ancient Greek *asulia*, which refers to protection by the gods.

4.

Like most contemporary nation-states, Greece the country began with a story, with a dream—and with a map.

The first map of what is now known as Greece was made in 1797 by a Greek exile named Rigas Velestinlis. By then, the glory of the ancient Greek city-states was a thing of the distant past, and the Ottomans had held sway over the region for nearly three and a half centuries. But Rigas, a student of the French Revolution, wanted his homeland to break free.

As a young man, Rigas had been accused of killing an Ottoman official and fled the empire, arriving, eventually, in Vienna, home to a large community of Greek exiles like him. Here, he edited a Greek-language newspaper to drum up support for his revolutionary ideas of an independent Greece, drafted a constitution for the proposed country, and drew his map. This map, explains the scholar Vangelis Calotychos, was less a representation of reality than it was an idea—a wish for what an independent nation-state called "Greece" could be.

Rigas was able to garner support for his fantasy of an independent Greece in part because of the recent vogue for ancient Greece—or for the idea of what it had once been. After the Renaissance had resurrected classical teachings, iconographies, and ideals, the eighteenth century saw a fascination with antiquity entering the mainstream. Northern Europeans began traveling to Greece in droves, as if on pilgrimage—much as I would, hundreds of years later. For them, the idealized fantasy of its more perfect past made it a "symbolic capital" for all of Europe.

Yet eighteenth-century Greece, and Greeks, bore little resemblance to the classical past as imagined by these outsiders. The region was poor, the majority of its people uneducated peasants; the glorious buildings of yore were, of course, mere ruins now. The travelers who came there from across Europe in search of the classical past denigrated its present-day inhabitants; "regular attributes of the 'modern Greeks' in the travellers' accounts," writes Beaton, "are deceitfulness and trickery." In this way, the obsession with ancient Greece, according to Calotychos, "obliged modern Greeks to assume a 'white man's burden' of their own, the racial impurity of not living up to the West's image of them."

Myths can serve as both mirror and invention—a guide to a culture's mores but also a willful fantasy of what it might be, what has not yet been born. Rigas's map made use of both. It was short on cartography, long on iconography. Like the Parthenon walls, its margins were filled with images of Greek gods and allusions to myths and military conquests from long ago. Rigas knew what he was doing. It was exiles like him, Calotychos posits, "who sought to weave the modern Greek story into the master narrative of European identity through allusion to the classical past and its ideals." Greece the contemporary place meant nothing to the rest of Europe without its history, but within its history, many had come to believe, was the dawn of Europe itself. And this myth would bolster another: of Greece as a fixed place with a border that defined and protected the heirs of its heritage—"the Greeks"—and kept foreigners out.

Rigas didn't live to see his map made manifest. In 1798, he and his comrades were captured by the Ottoman authorities, taken to Belgrade, and strangled in Nebojša Tower, their bodies heaved into the Danube below. "I have sown a rich seed," he was said to have proclaimed just before his death. "The hour is coming when my country will reap its glorious fruits." It is impossible to know whether he really uttered these words. In death, Rigas himself had become an idea, an ideal. Future generations would look to him as a hero, a martyr, an inspiration. When Greece finally did win its independence from the Ottomans in 1822 (thanks, in large part, to western Europe's enchantment with the origin story Rigas helped promote), the shape of the new country is not so far off from the nation-state Rigas had sketched on that first revolutionary map.

No matter how often I consulted maps on my phone and in guidebooks, I spent a ton of time utterly lost in Greece. In Athens, I found myself heading north just when I was certain I'd been southbound, ending up at one metro station when I'd meant to reach another, looping in circles when I could have sworn I was walking in a straight line. I would redouble my efforts to stay faithful to the maps, attempting, like a reverse cartographer, to graft the clues of its two-dimensional plane onto the many-dimensional world of Greece. But still, I almost never found my way with ease.

A map is only as good as a person's ability to follow it, yet there was another issue: in Greece, I often encountered maps that seemed incomplete, maps that excluded certain landmarks and overemphasized others, maps with routes that were clear enough on the page but confounded me in the landscape. For even the best of maps is merely an approximation of where you are and where you're trying to go. I got lost again while driving in the borderlands, lost on my little tourist pilgrimage to Delphi, lost all over Lesbos and in the Moria camp remains—lost, even, on the

Acropolis hill. Perhaps it was because I was only partly standing in the present, obsessed as I was with the markings and murmurs of the past. I was repeatedly struck by how quickly one reality yielded to another in the city, the ancient giving way to the modern, crumbling edifices to gleaming new construction, poverty to high-end commerce, bustle to utterly silent streets on which I was alone.

I understood that within each map lurks a fundamental paradox: it is both an attempted portrait of the world and a distortion of it. "A good map tells a multitude of little white lies," writes the cartographer Dr. Mark Monmonier in *How to Lie with Maps*. "It suppresses truth to help the user see what needs to be seen." Above all, maps revealed the way their maker understood the world—or how they wanted it to be understood by others. In this way, to read a map is necessarily to be manipulated, for a map can never truly match the world.

Many of the earliest human maps, I learned, were drawn on the walls of caves, painted onto tablets of clay, carved into mammoth tusks. I longed to see them firsthand. Early maps most often depicted villages and the topographical features—mountains, rivers, forests—of the mapmaker's universe. The very first maps, however, painted onto cave walls during the last Ice Age, were of the night sky. After all, people map what is most essential in their world. The alignment of the celestial bodies had long told people on earth how to live—when to plant, when to harvest, when the days would grow long and when short; like oracles, the stars held clues to what fate had in store.

The oldest surviving attempt to map the world is a Babylonian atlas painted on a clay tablet around 600 BCE. Not long after, the Greek Anaximander published the earliest surviving map of the world, a circular atlas that featured three continents—Europe, Asia, and Libya—divided by the Mediterranean, either the Tanais or the Phasis River, and the Nile and surrounded by ocean. In his theory of things, the earth was a circle, floating in space, as if, hundreds of years BCE, Anaximander, though limited by his era's understanding of the earth, had already intuited that we were a planet hovering in a greater galaxy of the cosmos.

In ancient times, people used the stars to navigate to faraway lands. Beneath the familiar landmarks of the night sky, wanderers could find their way. This method fused science and magic, but science, as it often does, left true magic behind as stargazing gave way to technologies of greater precision—navigating by latitude and longitude, the astrolabe, the mariner's compass. And these technologies in turn led to more elaborate, ambitious maps and atlases, which are themselves instruments of way-finding, of storytelling, and of dominion.

Every map is the product of a cartographer with allegiances. A map can easily mislead a person into believing that a certain landmass is larger or smaller than it really is; maps can also proclaim that a border is fixed when it is, in truth, under dispute. The mapmaker's choice of color, symbols, scale, and place names are all part of the illusory work of transposing a complex, three-dimensional world, with its attendant human drama and jockeying for power, onto a two-dimensional plane.

Maps were critical to Hitler's project, for instance, allowing him to render Germany as a small, aggrieved nation on certain maps while portraying it on others as an unstoppable force of global domination. In what Monmonier calls acts of "cartographic mischief," empires like the Soviet Union deliberately created false and confusing maps to thwart their enemies—for example, by placing a small town called Logashkino in a different location each time, sometimes by a river, sometimes on the sea—so that these maps could not be reliably used to plan attacks. Maps were critical to enacting Manifest Destiny in the United States, by giving form to unseen terrain and thus encouraging settlers to make their way westward. As John F. Ross explains in *The Promise of the Grand Canyon*, the white surveyors of the West served as "explainers and interpreters of lands that defied easy understanding, and had yet to find purchase in the American imagination." A map can enact new mythologies, for while mapping is a technology, it is also a canvas of imagination, subterfuge, blunder, and lie. In this way, writes Monmonier, "the map is the perfect symbol of the state."

For the state itself is an imaginary being. "Greece," "the United States," and "Afghanistan": these are just ideas that have been assigned a name and a perimeter.

Consider how Afghanistan came to be. The Afghans themselves had little say over the ultimate shape and scope of their country—over who, geopolitically, they were to become. The Great Game, as it came to be known, between the Russian and the British Empires, rendered the region both a pawn and a buffer zone between Russia and colonial India. Throughout the nineteenth century, the British went to war in Afghanistan to stave off Russian advances. When the powers finally agreed to a truce, they formed a joint commission to determine the country's northern borders. Later, the eastern border was drawn by Sir Henry Mortimer Durand, Britain's designee, and Afghan leader Abdur Rahman Khan. The British were adamant about securing strategic access to the Khyber Pass; Khan did what he could to negotiate his own interests and those of Afghanistan. The resulting border—christened "the Durand Line," making it clear that the imperial outsiders largely controlled the map—split Pashtun communities in two, causing much strife for the separated communities and ongoing territory disputes between Afghanistan and what would become Pakistan. Much of the country's enduring instability is a direct result of the way it was fixed onto the atlas.

Under European imperialism, to map a place was to claim it as territory. Early such maps were often elaborately drawn and adorned, as much works of art and invention as they were representations of actual geography. To leave an empty space was taboo, so mapmakers filled in what they did not know with decorative compass roses, outsize topographical features, and mythical beasts—ornate lions and sea monsters and dragons—as if to cover up both what was unknown and the fact of not knowing. Perhaps, posits the historian Chet Van Duzer, this tendency was a result of horror vacui, the artist's fear of empty space on the page. But horror vacui is also a fear of emptiness itself. The Europeans wondered what terrors lay in these unmapped, unseen spaces far away. They could only imagine—and by venturing into the spaces painted with monsters on the maps, they set in motion generations of war and subjugation and flight, bringing the truly monstrous to life.

When today's refugees arrive in Greece, they sometimes have no idea where on earth they've landed. The smugglers hadn't provided Ali and his shipmates with any kind of map; they'd merely pointed to a vague spot in the distance and told the helmsman, himself a refugee, to keep the boat aimed in that direction. Their landing point could have been anywhere in the Aegean, depending on where the whims of the wind and tide dragged them. Europe, Greece: just vague destinations, just words. It wasn't until the authorities told them where they were—Lesbos—that Ali was able to locate himself on the world map.

Though I have reported on borders all over the world, I had until my first trip to Greece dedicated most of my focus to the border between the United States and Mexico—a line on the map that resulted from centuries of imperialist genocide and theft, and which in turn set in motion centuries of further racist, lethal exclusion. Greece's borders, with their own histories and topographies, functioned much the same way, as did the rhetoric around them, and its effects. I knew before going to Greece that at least a million refugees had arrived in Greece by sea alone in recent years, with several thousand having died or gone missing, the sea a liquid cemetery—or, as a popular meme would later put it, "a crime scene." This was not so different from our own border, where hundreds of thousands of Central Americans and others had lost their lives attempting to cross the desert or the Rio Grande. And as in many parts of the United States, the impact of anti-refugee politics in Greece was evident nearly everywhere we went.

On my first trip to Athens, Ben and I rented an apartment right off the main square in Exarchia, a neighborhood known for its anarchists and artist squats and clashes between the left and the police. It was also rapidly gentrifying. This square became our cartographical reference point when trying to find our way home. It was surrounded by sundry shops and cafés and served as a hangout for a few dozen young men from Afghanistan. As in the States, the majority of the asylum seekers were young men, many of them minors traveling alone. In the square by our Athens apartment, the young men set up crates on the sidewalk where they chatted, smoked cigarettes, studied their phones, and watched the street as the rest of the world went by.

No matter how early we left each morning, they were already gathered in the square, some looking like they had just awoken, others as though they hadn't yet slept. They were still there when we returned. They spoke Dari, a language we recognized easily from our work with refugee families in California, Ben at a nonprofit he'd founded, me at the high school for immigrant youth where I'd worked as an administrator for over a decade. Each time we passed, I noticed in myself an urge to talk to them. Why, or to what end? My work as a journalist made me always want to ask questions, but journalism, I had come to recognize, is often an industry of extraction, no matter what we tell ourselves. My work as an educator was predicated on the idea that I could be of some help. I could connect people with lawyers, emergency housing support, food, mental health clinicians, educational opportunities. But I was far from home, with little to offer here. So we only waved and walked on.

It wasn't just this one square. Athens was filled with people stranded in the protracted purgatory of forced migration—refugees who, to make ends meet, sold bracelets they'd made or tickets to musical events, who squatted in encampments and lined up for food or for an audience inside one NGO office or another. Most refugees had landed in Greece in order to transit farther north into Europe, but in 2015 those countries quickly began sealing up their borders, like cascading dominoes: they erected fences and built walls and ultimately enforced the policy requiring refugees to remain in the first EU country in which they'd set foot. This meant that the better-resourced countries of the north were doing far less than Greece and Italy to support the growing number of people seeking safety in Europe every day. While the physical topography of Europe hadn't changed, for those seeking safety the map had been redrawn, most of its borders now impenetrable black lines.

If Rigas's map sought to define an inside—an *us* within the perimeters of an imagined homeland—contemporary borders emphasize the opposite: the *them* that exists outside increasingly fortified lines. For one of the fundamental tensions of our current age is that between estrangement and belonging—whether we are pining for a homeland real or imagined, safely secured within a walled country, or trying desperately to breach the wall. What was playing out in Greece today were the troubled questions of a globalized world: how the world changes and how we change with it, who belongs where, and how one is permitted across the ever-shifting lines of the state.

The young men in the square troubled me, the bitter look about them, the fact that this country could be at once a vacationer's paradise for some and effectively a prison for others who had committed no crimes. There were two young men in particular whom I saw day in and day out. They seemed to spend the better part of each day seated on crates in the square in a state of jittery unease, staring blankly, as if a red light had been switched on somewhere behind their eyes. They were outsiders, it was clear, and their treatment by the Greek government was meant to remind them and everyone else of this at each turn, as if they were artifacts on display in the museum of the city, or warnings.

After the economic crisis of 2008, an ultra-nationalist party called Golden Dawn that had first formed in the 1980s began to take firmer root in Greece. To them, Greece was a place of a single race—the Greek race, descended from the glorious leaders of yore. Like the Renaissance thinkers, Golden Dawn considered ancient Greece to have been the dawn of civilization, and it called for the rebirth of what its members considered to be a lost nation. Under their guidance, they claimed, Greece would rise again.

As the refugees began arriving in higher numbers, Golden Dawn's terrible ideology spread like rust. "The Europe of nations is back," Nikolaos Michaloliakos, the party's leader proclaimed. "Greece is only the beginning." In the olive grove hinterlands north of Athens, Golden Dawn trained its ragtag paramilitary troops and stockpiled arms. Members patrolled port towns and immigrant neighborhoods, stabbing and beating people they felt belonged elsewhere—outside Greek borders.

Eventually some of their members were voted into Parliament, where they sported Nazi-like regalia during official Parliament business. Though they deny links to Nazism, Golden Dawn's logo so closely resembles a swastika it could easily be mistaken for one at first glance, though it is in fact a meander symbol, named for the Meandros River—which now flows within the map of Türkiye. Golden Dawn's leaders have also been documented giving the Nazi salute, and the eagle on their flag resembles the eagle used by the Third Reich. (Just as the Third Reich borrowed iconography from Tibet and ancient Greece, contemporary Greek nationalists borrow iconography from the Nazis—a referential cycle of endless return.)

Until its leaders were found guilty of running a criminal organization in 2021 and its top leaders jailed, Golden Dawn would convene each year at Thermopylae, where, in 480 BCE, a small army of Greeks managed to stave off an advancing Persian army for several days. The symbolic fit of this valorous myth, however, was off—for the Greeks had ultimately lost the battle and were forced into retreat.

Rigas's dreams have largely come true: Greece is an independent country now, with a border, and the myths and histories sketched along his map's perimeter remain central to the broader project of Western identity. For perhaps mapmaking is a matter of rendering into two dimensions not just three dimensions but also a fourth—the fourth being its political topography: that is, what we've chosen a place to mean and stand for.

"This route does not exist on a map," a Congolese man once told me of the overland journey he had taken from Brazil to Mexico. The fact that the route did not exist on a map was the very thing that allowed tens of thousands of migrants like him to make the trip each year, US-bound: they could move for long distances undetected. But this unmapped journey required traversing deadly territory through punishing jungles and fast-running rivers, where thieves lay in wait and unscrupulous guides left their charges for dead and absconded with the money they'd been paid to escort them to safety. Such is the thin, shaky line contemporary migrants must follow in a world determined by borders: to be too lost is to risk death, but to be found is to risk being captured, which can itself be a death sentence. You have to be just lost enough to save your life.

5.

Ali had crossed border after border, working hard to keep his bearings while also attempting to fly under the radar of the various law enforcement and border authorities, his eyes trained on the horizon of the future. Again and again, he found himself pleading to God for protection: in Iran, in Türkiye, adrift on the Aegean, and once he was inside what had come to be known as "Fortress Europe." He also needed help from mortals on earth.

But gone were the days of *asulia* among the ancients; gone, too, were the early days of 2015, when Greeks had so vigorously welcomed those seeking refuge by land and sea, when fishermen patrolled for shipwrecks and grannies made meals for the refugees to have something to eat when they landed onshore and Greeks from all over the country headed to the islands to work in solidarity with the new arrivals. So vigorous had the welcome been that in 2015, two Greeks from Lesbos, a grandma and a fisherman, were nominated for a Nobel Peace Prize for representing the "behavior and attitude of Greece, organizations and volunteers towards the huge refugee crisis." But over time, many locals grew weary of the new arrivals, and politicians—mainstream ones, not just the fringe elements of Golden Dawn—had stoked the flames. Greece couldn't be a destination for just any kid in Afghanistan living in poverty, the government admonished. Poverty was not grounds for asylum, they reminded their citizens. And above all: Why the Greeks? Why wasn't the rest of Europe doing its part to house the refugees?

"Greece can no longer be a convenient parking lot for refugees headed to Europe," Prime Minister Mitsotakis announced in 2019, the year Ali arrived. At the same time, the Greek government began instituting shadow policies to keep refugees from being able to cross at all.

Travelers of another kind, however, were beckoned to Greece—a country where tourism accounts for nearly 20 percent of the GDP. I may have been on a quest, but in technical terms I was a tourist, the kind of traveler Greece wanted: someone with money and a passport, someone who might post pictures of their trip online that would in turn lure others just like them.

A few days after our wanderings in Anafiotika, Ben and I were desperate for a break from Athens's heat. So we set out for the islands one day, cramming into the hold of a low-riding ferry called the *Flying Dolphin*. We docked in Hydra's tranquil horseshoe harbor, where elaborately festooned donkeys stood at attention, waiting to be loaded up with goods and suitcases and hotel guests. There were hardly any cars on the island, only these donkeys and the occasional golf cart. There was also limited fresh water; much of the island's supply is processed in desalination plants or has to be shipped in. But Hydra was the heavenly Greece I'd seen in pictures: women dressed in sun hats and linen sheaths, shady cafés, whitewashed stone buildings, beaches punctuating the rocky coastline—a place of buoyancy and ease, as if the island itself were afloat and drifting.

We ate breakfast by the pier while studying a rudimentary tourist map, its pathways drawn in thick, cartoonish blue and red lines. If we continued down the southern side of the island for a few miles we would pass a number of beaches; if we kept going, it seemed, we could hook eastward, taking the long way back to town on a path that skirted more remote coastline and the base of Mount Eros, which we could summit if we felt up for an extra climb. This loop, which we estimated to be about six miles, would take us through a series of small towns that dotted the map like a string of beads. The route looked straightforward, and we estimated it would take us only a couple of hours, leaving plenty of time before our ferry home. We finished our breakfast, I slurped the last of my coffee, and we asked our waitress, somewhat bashfully, if we might fill our two small water bottles from the restaurant's tap before setting off.

The first few miles followed an easy stone pathway along the sea, past restaurants and cafés, the shoreline speckled with bathers. Eventually the path turned to dirt, then arrived at a small, south-facing harbor. There were no people there, no shops or restaurants, only a half-dozen spare houses and some boats bobbing near shore. We knew the road wound uphill from that point, so we decided to jump into the sea once more before our ascent. The cool, clear water enveloped us like a salve. But as we swam, I noticed that the bleached rocks beneath us were studded with black urchins, their spiny silhouettes catching light through the water, winking at us like sinister jewels. I insisted that we dog-paddle up the boat ramp until we were nearly to shore so as not to accidentally step on them. That was me: despite my privilege and good fortune—or maybe because my line of work made me hyperaware of it—I was always bracing for danger and disaster.

Ben rolled his eyes, but he went along with it. Although he did similar work, he wasn't so preoccupied with personal doom. Instead he tended to be bereft about the state of the world and in particular of the ailing sea, which often featured in his poems. The previous summer, we'd taken a walk on a beach in California, where, because the ocean had warmed so dramatically the week before, millions of mussels had boiled alive. He'd drafted a poem as we walked, the shore littered with their opened shells: *Pelagic, coated / in a thin layer of film, / the soft body of a mollusk / shares myriad traits / with the human tongue.* Like war, climate change was also evicting people from their homes.

After our swim, we dried off and continued along the path—or what we thought was the path. We passed a few houses—simple boxlike structures made mostly of cinder block and stone. Some had windowpanes, others did not. The gardens were dry and mostly overgrown. Through one window we saw a ruddy-faced man sitting alone at a plastic card table, drinking a can of beer as if it were his solemn duty. His eyes raised to meet ours but lowered again before we could wave. Soon the path turned to brush. We tried another route; that, too, led nowhere.

"There it is," Ben said, pointing up the hill to where a road cut clean as a lance through the yellowed grasses. We walked toward it, but it vanished in no time. Where the path should have been lay only more rocks and brittle brush that, when the breeze came, hissed like snakes. We turned back toward the harbor, passing the man in the window, who was now on his second can of beer. Again we spotted the road up ahead but again it disappeared, leaving us in a confounding nowhere. I drank some water from our supply. The man walked out of his house, a knapsack slung over his shoulder.

"Episkopi?" he said, which we recognized as the name of the town at the top of the hill on our map. *Yes,* we told him, *yes, Episkopi, yes.* He showed us the way—so easy, so smoothly found that we couldn't quite figure out how we'd ever managed to be lost. We thanked him and set off up the hill through a cooling thicket of pines. Our bottles were almost empty, but we'd purchase more water once we reached Episkopi. The houses we passed seemed long abandoned, as if from another century—or perhaps from a time when this country wasn't drowning in debt. *For Sale*, read a hand-scrawled sign in both Greek and English. Soon, there were no houses at all.

At the top of the hill, the forest emptied us onto a broad, dry escarpment with a view of the sea in all directions. Episkopi was closer to a ruin than a town, with only a few stone houses, and winding walls of piled rock—delineating what, we weren't sure. There was no one else around, and certainly no water for sale. I'd had too much coffee earlier, and now our bottles were empty, the sun lavishing itself upon us from above. My head was starting to hurt. Ben explored the cliffs while I found some shade in the town's collapsing, three-walled chapel. I closed my eyes but was soon startled by a sudden racket. A herd of goats was running in my direction, bells clanging against their throats. My presence had startled them. They turned back toward the ghost town and disappeared.

Farther on, we encountered a group of tourists, also from the States, coming from the direction we were headed. "It's quite a hike," one of them said, eyeing my outfit: a sundress, black Converse sneakers I'd bought years ago at a consignment shop for eight bucks. "You guys gonna be okay?"

I resented the suggestion—I was more rugged than I looked. "We're good," Ben insisted on our behalf. They offered us water but we politely refused, claiming they needed it as much as we did.

We resumed our march over an open terrain of low scrub. It was roughly one o'clock by now, with no shade to be found. We'd been hiking for three hours. Perhaps we'd find another town—one with water—up ahead. At the base of the cliffs far below was a pristine, shady beach where a few swimmers floated alongside an anchored water taxi, its bright red stripe jarring and unreal in this landscape of scrub and thirst. We considered taking the path down there, as if somewhere between them and us was a hatch through which we could slip off this sizzling moonscape and back into the day we had imagined for ourselves, all levity and ease. But the beach was about a mile and a half away. We had no cell service. What if the boats were gone by the time we made it down? We kept going, walking another mile and then another across the baked earth, encountering no one. I thought of the tourists, our stupid refusal of their water.

We descended and summited, descended and summited again, Ben moving effortlessly ahead. Anytime we stopped, ravenous green horseflies swarmed us and bit. My head was pounding now. We looked at the map again: after another two hours, we seemed to be where I thought we'd been hours before. We had so much farther to go.

"You'll be okay," Ben said. "You got this." I thought of some lines from *The Waste Land*, something about rock and no water and stopping to drink, but I couldn't recall the exact order of the words.

Eventually another crumbling church came into view. I leaned against its back wall, trying to shrink myself enough to disappear into its thin triangle of shade. I was woozy, my eyesight blurred with splotches of black. My legs were wobbly. I'd hardly been seated an instant before I spontaneously started to pee, unable to stop myself.

"You peed?" Ben said. This sometimes happened, he knew from his marathon days, when the body began to shut down, but he didn't say this to me. I laughed, and we studied the terrible map, but I could tell he was worried. All the towns we had imagined we'd walk through turned out to be just this: disintegrating stones, stray goats, some unconjurable past. There'd be no water. By my calculations, we were about two and a half miles away from the town of Hydra. Only another hour or so without a drink. Ben issued no correction.

Near the base of Mount Eros ("Want to head up there?" Ben joked, pointing to the barren peak), we began sloping slightly downhill—finally, I thought, toward town. The way narrowed and narrowed some more, and the farther we walked, the more the sides of the path began to close in on themselves, as if in some elaborate act of vanishing. The spiny brush caught against my legs, drawing blood. I felt something move against my face and I jolted backward, snatching it from my cheek. "What's wrong?" Ben asked as I opened my hand, revealing an enormous black spider, its body the size of a nickel, its legs sleek and knuckled as if armor-clad. It felt like a tiny omen. Around every corner, it seemed, was a new surprise, a new mystery, a new problem. I flung the spider into the brush. What other signs did we need that we'd slipped into some other realm, into a current of sinister unreal?

The more we walked, the more spiders we encountered; their webs stretched across the narrowing path, and we had to bend and duck to avoid becoming ensnared. Surely no one had walked this webbed trail for some time. Where were we?

Soon the path vanished yet again. We'd clearly made a wrong turn somewhere. I took a seat. On cue, the horseflies appeared. Ben set off to figure out where we'd gone wrong and how to meet back up with the trail. Who knew how long we'd been walking astray? I was now alone atop the scrub, the horseflies feasting on my legs. I was too weary to swat them. I know how pathetic that sounds, and I knew it then. But the truth was I could barely move my arms. I closed my eyes, imagining the darkness behind my lids was a kind of shade, and fell asleep while the flies feasted.

Here is no water but only rock
Rock and no water and the sandy road
The road winding above among the mountains
Which are mountains of rock without water
If there were water we should stop and drink
Amongst the rock one cannot stop or think

I lurched awake. I called for Ben, but was immediately unsure if I'd made much of a sound. So I gathered my strength and screamed his name. Nothing. I pictured him getting bitten by a snake, twisting his ankle and falling down the hill, hitting his head. What would I be able to do to help him? Wasn't this a common story—moronic tourists lose their way, meet their end? I knew a writer who died of heatstroke on assignment: a young man, strong, an adventurer in body and spirit. Within just a few minutes of passing out, he was dead. Where the hell was Ben? Where the hell was I? I thought of all the young people I knew who had told me about being lost in the desert en route to their US destinations, the brutal disorientation of it, and these thoughts made me feel terribly ashamed that I would now, hovering above this paradise and fleeing nothing—just a little too hot, a little too thirsty, and all of my own doing—feel any fear at all.

Finally, Ben reappeared. "I was shouting for you!" I practically screamed.

"I was shouting for *you*!" he replied. He hadn't been able to find his way back to me and had called and called my name. Hadn't I heard him?

He hadn't been all that far. But here the rules of ordinary reality did not apply.

"We can either bushwhack," he reported, pointing to the vast thicket that dropped steeply down below, "or head back uphill and try to find the trail." I looked at the thicket, thought again of snakes. We turned around to find the trail. At the top of the hill, the town of Hydra came into view—so close, so far. But soon the path vanished again and I began to tremble.

"I'm just going to sit here in this shade," I announced, motioning to a two-foot-high stone wall, "while you go find the path." Ben looked away. (Later he would tell me that there'd been no shade at all; I'd conjured a mirage.) He took off up the hill toward an abandoned-looking lean-to that appeared to have once been some kind of stable. Inside was a cracked basin. Ben inspected it, but I could see from his face that it was empty. If there had been anything in it, I would have drunk it. I would have drunk anything.

If there were rock
And also water
And water
A spring
A pool among the rock
If there were the sound of water only
Not the cicada
And dry grass singing

My frailty felt political, and it was. My passport, my credit card, and my whiteness permitted this frailty, and even facilitated it, along with my stupidity in taking this hike in the first place so unprepared. I had come to this country to better understand the contemporary refugee crisis and my own family's origin story, and to study the manner in which the myths of whiteness and of "Western civilization" influenced both. Clarity and answers were what I'd been searching for, but instead I found myself twisting round and round—upon the questions, upon the landscape itself. Here I was lost, in the pitiless terrain of my ancestors that had also given form to the canonical Greek myths—those stories of heroic journey and vigorous punishment, that elaborate pantheon of gods and beasts. "Neither Hera nor Athena nor Zeus are the things which those who consecrate temples and walls to them consider them to be," wrote the Epicurean philosopher Metrodorus of Lampsacus, "but they are manifestations of nature and arrangements of the elements." These ancient myths were just lessons passed through the generations: an explanation of the physical world and a set of instructions—a map, one might say—for how to live, how to survive. That's what made the new, political myths taking root all the more terrifying: the possibility that people would begin to live according to their teachings.

Eventually we found a way. We descended the hill on what appeared to be a goat trail. The closer the town came into view, the more I disbelieved, as if any minute the trail would shoot us back up again, the town slipping once more from our sight. But soon we were walking past inhabited houses upon a veritable stone path, which then became a road that led to still more houses, their lush, manicured gardens some insistence of civilization. Ben quickly began knocking on doors to ask for water, but no one answered. After several houses, he found a hose. I held my breath as he turned the tap. Water—it flowed so easily, as if it were nothing. I drank greedily, then handed the hose to Ben, and we traded like this, gasping and sucking, for several minutes. "Let's go," he said once our bottles were filled. He had some notion that we might make the ferry and get the hell out of there. But even I, from within my heatstroke, knew that our ferry was long gone. There was no rush now, and I knew I needed to leave an offering of some kind.

I rummaged around in my backpack for a few coins, which I placed gently by the tap, offering a silent, sun-addled prayer before turning around to catch up to Ben. I was back across the threshold of the living.

Soon we were at the harbor once again. The boats bobbed, the tourists licked their gelato, the elderly men drank their coffee unhurried, women entered and exited the air-conditioned shops with their parcels, skirts billowing behind them.

It was half past five. The next ferry wasn't until nine. We bought water, then two overpriced lemonades, and then two more lemonades, and walked down to one of the rocky beaches. We jumped into the water, the chill of it so abrupt it felt as though our skin might harden onto us like lava. We were afloat in the sea now, immersed in an oceanic gratitude.

It turned out that we had walked nearly fifteen miles in ninety-degree heat with only two small bottles of water. I felt ashamed at our unpreparedness, at how narrowly I'd passed whatever test I'd been given. Ben changed into pants and I pulled on the black silk dress that had spent the day stuffed in the bottom of our backpack. Like that, we were transformed.

We found a restaurant that overlooked the sea and ate a luxurious meal, napkins on our laps, plates arranged so nicely, ice-cold water in tall-stemmed glasses. It was so easy for us to slip from one reality into another, to slip across the line.

We paid the bill. There was still some time before the ferry took off, so we sat on the edge of a cliff, watching as the horizon hauled down the sun like a sail. But a Hydra, I was reminded, is a many-headed snake. Just as we were feeling ourselves again, one of those muscular black spiders dropped mere inches from our faces, hovering on its glossy thread so that it was perfectly silhouetted by the blazing orange sun.

6.

It wasn't only on Hydra; all over Greece, homes stood half constructed, once-thriving businesses lay empty, buildings seemed to crumble toward dust. The global economic crisis had nearly destroyed Greece in 2008, and although things had improved, the effects remained.

After the collapse, the powers of the Eurozone had orchestrated a "bailout" that relieved northern European banks of Greece's debt, transferred the burden to European taxpayers, and effectively hitched Greece to an endless debt regime. The Greek government, which had been rife with corruption and mismanagement that protected wealthy oligarchs, was forced to adopt austerity measures. *This country is run by a mafia,* Demetrios had said. It was clear that there was no path for the national debt ever to be repaid. In 2010, for every $100 of income a Greek made, the state owed $146 to foreign banks.

According to the scholar Vangelis Calotychos, the financial crisis that still besieges Greece is explained partly by the vast chasm between modern and classical Greece, or what the dominant historical narrative insists the place once was. "The denigration of modern Greece, its material manifestation," he writes, "is a by-product of attaining the Ideal of Greece"—that ideal that Rigas fashioned in a map. In other words, Greece must giddily enact its classical heritage in order to maintain legitimacy within the European project. For though the rest of Europe and the so-called West regards Acropolis-era Greece as a historical, intellectual, and moral wellspring, it routinely dismisses contemporary Greece as a wayward country of the periphery, Greeks as western Europe's lazy, corrupt, darker-skinned southern cousins.

"Our country's fiscal waterboarding," wrote Yanis Varoufakis, the former finance minister, of the debt regime imposed on Greece, "was celebrated as a sensible way of bringing lost people back into the fold."

Greek leaders must constantly declare their allegiance to their imagined origins, and must perform this version of "Greekness" for "the West." "There is no greater honor for the elected leader of the people who created democracy," Prime Minister Mitsotakis told the US Congress in 2022, "than to address the elected representatives of the people who founded their country on the Greek model and have promoted and defended democratic values ever since."

Like Rigas, Mitsotakis played the past like an instrument. The invocation of classical Greece—*we and you, we are the same, and in fact you come from us,* Mitsotakis was suggesting to the US lawmakers—sought to secure what had been a precarious legitimacy within the respectability politics of western and northern Europe (and thus by extension the United States). It also sought to obscure the fact that Greece, with its rampant corruption, widespread poverty, and increasing autocratic leanings, now defied its own origin story. Today's regional politics suggest that in order for Greece to be fully European, it must above all defend Europe's borders from the refugees.

There's a cost to this performance. During the early days of the Greek debt crisis, an epidemic of suicides began. Seventy-seven-year-old Dimitris Christoulas was a retired pharmacist in Athens whose pension was cut and then cut again as a result of government austerity measures.

Eventually he couldn't afford even his own medicine—a prescription he needed in order to live. One April morning in 2012, Christoulas went to busy Syntagma Square, walked to a spot beneath a tree, pulled out a gun, and announced, "Don't leave debts to your children." He then shot himself in the head.

"I see no other solution than this dignified end to my life," Christoulas wrote in the note he left behind, "so I don't find myself fishing through garbage cans for my sustenance."

Between 2010 and 2012, Greece's suicide rate rose 35 percent. Those who killed themselves were most often working-age men and retirees living off already meager pensions, particularly those who, like Christoulas, were most likely to lose their jobs or have their salaries or pensions cut, were less able to leave the country for greener pastures, and had a shorter horizon upon which things could once again turn right. It wasn't so much that people didn't have anything to live for anymore, though the economic crisis had taken much from them. Suicide, as Christoulas's note suggested, was a response to their sudden change of circumstances, and their shame.

"Like all other suicides," said Christoulas's daughter, "it was a political murder."

"Malicious vulgar poverty," thinks a character in a short story by the contemporary Greek writer Christos Ikonomou, whose work has chronicled the financial crisis. "It too has become a creature of the house. A creature of the house, a pet rat."

Young Greeks began to leave the country in droves. More than 500,000 people emigrated from Greece between 2008 and 2016—more in those eight years than in the great Greek migration of the early twentieth century, from which I am descended. This lost generation may never return. "It seems that Greece," writes Ikonomou, "has not only lost its present but its future, if we reflect that these people are the generation whose task it is (or ought to be) to find a concrete expression for the new vision of Greece: a country with a creative, productive economy and a just, functional state."

And then came 2015, when hundreds of thousands and then millions of people from Africa and Asia and the Middle East fled their own homes in search of safety in Europe, washing up sodden and desperate and sometimes dead on Greece's shores. Golden Dawn remained in Parliament, and had won seats in the European Parliament, too. Someone was to blame for this suffering, this loss in status. Many pointed to the northern Europeans; many others pointed to the refugees.

This is the context that brought Moria to life: a camp constructed in the still-roiling wake of the debt crisis that fleeced Greece and the Greeks, a camp necessitated by the European Union's regulations requiring all asylum seekers to register in the first country of arrival, a camp to warehouse the unwanted, a camp for whose wretched conditions everyone refused to take the blame.

By early 2020, seven years after the camp opened, Lesbos was seething. The islanders and the refugees and the international aid workers had all had enough, even if the source of their fury and frustrations differed. Left-wingers protested the summary detention of newly arrived refugees at the port of Mytilene, while right-wingers were outraged that refugees were still being housed en masse on the island at all. The central government sent riot police to quell the chaos, but they were met at the port by throngs of people all along the political spectrum—united, momentarily, against the central authorities. The protesters hurled insults and garbage cans at the police as they marched off the ship. Businesses shuttered in a strike, leaving the police without food to eat or hotels in which to sleep. After a few days, the police went back to Athens.

Then, at the beginning of March, in response to Türkiye's halted patrols, Greece announced that it was suspending asylum applications—in spite of the fact that this was against Greek and EU law. A group of far-right thugs began attacking aid workers, including a cadre of foreign doctors, beating people up and smashing their cars. The medical workers fled to the airport. "We left fearing for our lives," one doctor told *The Guardian.*

On March 23, the Greek government issued COVID-19 restrictions that closed Moria to the outside world for the rest of the spring and summer. No one was allowed to leave without special permission. Ali had effectively become an inmate now. He hunkered in the sweltering camp, his tent like a tandoor beneath the sun. The sea was right there, in walking distance; when there was a little wind, you could even smell the salt. The island opened to visitors from Europe that summer, in the hope of recuperating lost tourist euros, but Ali and the rest of the refugees remained confined inside Moria.

It was at the beginning of September that authorities discovered the first case of COVID in the camp. In January, there had been roughly 20,000 people living in Moria, but because of increased transfers and people self-smuggling off the island, Moria now housed roughly 11,000. There was still insufficient healthcare in the camp. As the virus spread and contact tracers did their work, dozens of residents were forced into quarantine facilities. Most NGOs were suspended from operating inside the camp. Whatever efforts were being made to keep Moria safe, they weren't effectively communicated to the residents. To most, they felt like just another set of punitive restrictions. Ali was afraid of what would happen next. "Many people felt they were being left to die," Amelia Cooper of Legal Centre Lesvos told me.

A few days after the COVID patients were put into isolation units, word got out that the local government was contracting with a local company to build a wall to encircle Moria, jungle and all, for good.

In spite of the confinement and the turmoil around him, 2020 wasn't entirely bad for Ali: in August, he had gotten word that his asylum interview was scheduled for mid-September. Meanwhile, his paperwork from Afghanistan had arrived, which would confirm his status as a minor and help his lawyers plead his case. August came and went, and there was no change to his interview date—a good sign.

The week before his interview, as he remembers it, Ali was visiting friends in Zone 4, a few hundred meters from where he lived, when he saw flames in the distance. There had been many fires before in Moria—some small, others deadly, as when, in 2019, a woman and her young son had burned to death in a flaming IsoBox before anyone could squelch the flames. But this fire was different. Already it seemed bigger than any he'd seen before. He headed back toward his tent and found his neighbors in a state of panic. All around him people were shouting, darting in and out of their tents, and packing their belongings. He grabbed the backpack where he kept his documents, stuffed a change of clothes inside, and ran toward the road leading to Mytilene.

The smell is what Ali remembers most. This was smoke, but nothing like the smell of a cook fire or a woodpile burning; it was the stench of human things on fire, things that weren't meant to burn. In the distance the fire was gaining speed as he and thousands of others flooded the main road, making their run for it. Though it was peak COVID, few wore masks. They were thinking only of escaping the fire, Ali recalls. But they didn't make it far. Soon they were stopped in their tracks, for the police had blocked passage into the city of Mytilene.

"Behind us was fire," one man told me of that night, "in front of us was police." The fascists had blocked the road leading in the other direction.

There was nowhere else to go, so Ali dropped his backpack on the tarmac and lay his head on it like a pillow. Everyone around him did the same. But he couldn't sleep. All he could think about was his approaching interview and how it would likely be rescheduled on account of the fire—how he'd be stuck on this island for longer still.

The next week, the streets leading from Moria camp were bedlam. The 11,000 refugees remained trapped there, sleeping beneath trees and in the local cemetery and fully exposed along the road. There was still no shelter and scant medical care; food and water appeared irregularly, and when they did, the delivery vans were swarmed. Citing security and COVID concerns, government officials blocked most NGOs from the area—even those offering food and sanitation services. When the refugees dared to protest these conditions, the police sprayed tear gas into the crowds and threatened further violence should they persist.

Meanwhile, the authorities scrambled to figure out a place to put the refugees. National officials felt it imperative to establish a new camp as soon as possible in order to send the message that the fire would not secure anyone transfers to the mainland or beyond Greece, as some rumors circulating through the roads claimed.

"We were very worried during the Moria fire that if we didn't find a solution very quickly, that could incentivize people to burn the rest of the camps," Notis Mitarachi, then the minister of migration, told me. While the government was indeed appealing to other nations to take some of the refugees, it didn't want to send the message that burning down a camp was a mechanism to leave the country. In other words, the government didn't want refugees to get the idea that any other reality but Moria was possible for them—or that they themselves could do anything to achieve it.

On September 12, the Ministry of Migration announced that a new facility would soon be opened on an old military base. The new camp was called Mavrovouni, which means "Black Mountain" in Greek. It was adjacent to a camp for those the UN deemed particularly vulnerable—people with physical disabilities, large families, single mothers—that the authorities had recently closed. That camp was called Kara Tepe—which, absurdly, meant "Black Hill" in Turkish.

Some refugees revolted at the news, fearing it would be Moria all over again. This led to more clashes with the police, and more tear gas.

It was during this time of chaos that Ali, asleep on the road, remembers being approached by the police. "Ali," they called, just his first name. He turned his head. "We want to talk to you," they told him, and asked him to follow them. He thought it might have something to do with his interview.

They walked him to the other side of the police barricades, then suddenly handcuffed him and loaded him into the police car. "What's going on?" he asked, stunned, but they didn't answer. Soon they were at the Mytilene police station, where the authorities accused him of starting the fire.

"It wasn't me," he recalls telling them. "I wasn't even around, I was way far away from where it started." But they weren't having it. *Who was with you?* they asked. *How did you do it?* Ali maintained his innocence.

Fine, he insists they said, *then give us six other names and we'll set you free.* But he wasn't about to name other people for something they didn't do, and he told the police as much.

"Okay, go and spend thirty years of your life in prison," they told him.

"I said, 'If I'm not guilty, fine, it's all right,'" he recalled to me. "'I'm not guilty, I didn't do anything.'" If they were going to falsely accuse him, what power did he have to stop them? "I don't want to put anyone in prison without any reason," he said. "So I'm not blaming anyone. I didn't see anyone light the fire."

Ali spent that night in a cell in the police station. The next day, others joined him. Soon there were six of them—the Moria 6, as they'd come to be known, all young Afghans accused of setting the fire.

Ali called his brother in California from the police station to tell him he'd been arrested.

"Did you do it?" his brother asked.

"No, I didn't do it, I'm innocent," Ali told him.

"Then don't worry," his brother said. This was Greece, after all—Europe, not Afghanistan, a place where the rule of law reigned. Greece was the birthplace of democracy, for heaven's sake, a place whose very origin story is steeped in ideas of justice. Ali's brother was certain that, soon enough, everything would be cleared up and Ali would be set free.

"If you didn't do it," he told Ali, "you have nothing to worry about."

PART II

Past

7.

"Moria camp burning," Vaselis the baker told me as he pulled bread from the oven, "was a gift from God." It was late morning in Moria town, and his baskets were brimming with loaves that he had baked and cooled. His mother, standing watch over the register, nodded. He pointed to my notebook and said it again: "Moria camp burning was a gift from God, and you can tell them that Vaselis Tsakiris of Moria town said so. Put that in your story."

The town of Moria is a stone village, home to fewer than a thousand people. It appears, as many old towns in Greece do, as it might have hundreds of years ago—its buildings draped with ivy and disintegrating in places, streets barely wide enough for a car to pass. Early on in the refugee crisis, most Moria townspeople felt for the refugees being housed less than a mile away, and welcomed them. They put out bottles of water, cooked large pots of food, donated clothing and toys for the children.

The problem, Vaselis explained, was that the refugees didn't stop coming. More arrived, and then more still. The conditions they lived in at the camp, he knew, were wretched, as were the situations they'd left behind. But three times, he told me—"Three times!" his mother emphasized from the register—his bakery had been broken into by refugees in search of food and money. Twice, they'd shattered the windows. Guess who'd had to pay for the repairs? Not the government, that's for sure, even though the government had warehoused the refugees here and was supposed to be responsible for them. Not the EU.

Vaselis pointed to a framed portrait of an elderly gentleman propped on a shelf above where his mother stood.

"That's my father," he said. Vaselis's father had come to Lesbos as a refugee from Asia Minor—Anatolia, now Türkiye—in 1922. His family had opened this bakery soon after. In its nearly hundred-year history there had never been a robbery, never a problem. Not a single one! Until the new refugees came.

Vaselis opened the oven and shut it again, spread flour over the counter, kneaded dough, and swiftly shaped it into a loaf. He held his shoulders stiff, and he never slowed. He was in such perpetual motion that he gave the impression that he might sleep on top of the blankets at night, fully clothed and ready to rise at any instant. As we chatted, villagers arrived by foot and car to yell their orders through the shop window. Vaselis's mother traded loaves for coins and waved them on.

An elderly gentleman pulled up on a motorbike for his daily bread. "Ask this man," Vaselis said, "ask this man about the refugees!"

With his motor still running, the man told me how residents of the camp had cut thirty olive trees from one of his fields and fourteen from another. The government had not yet compensated him for his loss; he was still waiting for the money so he could replant his trees. The man threw his hands up—nothing to be done—tucked the loaf under his arm, and sped away.

It wasn't really the refugees' fault, most villagers understood. Look at how they were treated, after all, how they were forced to live. But what about the people of Moria town? Weren't they to be considered in the geopolitical equation? Politicians would come to Lesbos from all over Europe, all over the world, Vaselis lamented, in order to visit the camp and make policy decisions, but never once would they pass through town to ask the villagers what they needed or how they felt about things—not even to buy a coffee or have some lunch or purchase some of Vaselis's warm bread.

We thanked Vaselis for his time and he handed me one of the ring-shaped koulouris, fresh from the oven. He wouldn't accept my money. As payment, he said, I could put this in my story, too: how delicious is the koulouri made by Vaselis of Moria town in Lesbos—this island on Europe's edge.

There were no physical walls separating Lesbos from what lay beyond, not yet, anyway. But politicians and residents were calling for such fortifications to be considered on the island, while also enacting immigration policies that served as their own forms of barricade. What would such a physical border accomplish? Border walls, suggests the political theorist Wendy Brown, are products of the kind of xenophobia that was taking root on Lesbos, but they can also create it. A walled-off country swells with what she calls imaginaries of insiders and outsiders, where the outside is brimming with "danger, criminality and foreignness" and the inside with a "fictional homogeneity, tranquility, sanctity and belonging."

"She looks Greek," Vaselis told my interpreter, Thanasis, as we turned to go, words that I understood without translation and that, absurdly, delighted me—the idea that I might be recognized as a wayward daughter, returned.

"Her great-grandmother came from Andros," Thanasis told Vaselis.

"Andros! That's good," Vaselis replied, and gave me a thumbs-up. Even though the island was in the Cyclades, hundreds of miles away, it was still Greece. But it was a real shame I didn't speak the language, he said. I agreed; it was a point of sorrow for me, particularly when in

Greece, that I knew just a paltry handful of words. My grandmother had spoken Greek, but only to her mother and her sister, and generally only when she was saying something she didn't want the rest of us to know. My father and his siblings never learned; the language had vanished from our lineage because of the commonly internalized idea that one must choose between the tongue of the homeland and that of the new country—language, too, a sacrifice of ascension. Thus, to me, Greek was and is a language of secrets: of closed doors, abandoned places, unspoken tragedies—and eventually, as a journalist, of an impenetrable bureaucracy keeping facts from view.

"My grandmother didn't teach me," I told the baker in English by way of excuse. He was shaking his head with disappointment even before Thanasis finished converting my words to Greek.

"You must come back one day," he said, "speaking Greek." His family and mine had something in common—a claim to being Greek, and an ancestry of uprooting that helped determine the way we saw the world and our place in it. My self-proclaimed Greekness, along with my whiteness and my apparent resources, rendered me insider enough. He handed me a loaf of warm bread and waved me on. With this, I was sanctified.

8.

In January 1914, several months before World War I began, my sixteen-year-old great-grandmother Evanthia, along with her mother, Fotini, and her little brother, Yiannis, left their Cycladic island of Andros and traveled through Athens to the port city of Patras. It was about two hundred miles as the crow flies, a days-long journey back then. Patras faced westward—toward New York, where they were headed—the starting point from which my ancestors, and so many Greeks like them, would eventually become Greek Americans.

This was modern Greece's first great outmigration. In the span of thirty years, 421,000 Greeks would leave home because of poverty and encroaching war. There were no reliable jobs to be had for my great-great-grandfather or for his children. "They treated us badly," was the simple explanation passed down through the generations for their leaving.

In Patras they boarded the SS *Ultonia*, a five-hundred-foot-long steel-hulled ship built in 1898 to transport cargo and cattle. As the market for voluntary transatlantic migration boomed, the *Ultonia* was converted into a passenger ship outfitted to carry up to twenty-two hundred people. It was nothing fancy; in fact, it looked a bit like a warship, its four masts trained toward heaven like bayonets. But it was tested on the wintry Atlantic swell. The ship held second-class berths for a hundred or so passengers; the other hundreds were crammed into third-class bunks, where they worked to keep themselves from falling seasick or going mad. (The trick, my grandmother taught me years later, as if passing on an heirloom, is to train your eyes on the horizon.) My family traveled third class, of course. If they could afford otherwise, why leave?

They arrived in New York in just under a month, docking at Ellis Island for processing. In New York it was day fifteen of a three-week cold snap, this new-to-them world draped in two feet of unfamiliar snow.

On the ship's manifest, Evanthia was logged as a "domestic," her mother a "housewife," ten-year-old "John" (Yiannis no more) a "scholar." The Ellis Island civil servant deemed these aliens to be of sound mental and physical health, then turned them loose on a world that wasn't theirs, that had itself been stolen centuries before their arrival. It was as if they'd touched down on another planet.

They headed to Boston and began working. A few years later, my great-grandmother married and had four children—two boys, Theodore the eldest and Nicky the youngest, and two girls: my grandmother Penelope and her younger sister, Tula. The sisters were radiant, and so alike that they were often mistaken for twins. Right after Nicky was born, Evanthia's husband died. Now a single mother raising four kids alone, she found work managing a Greek diner in New Haven called the Belle Spa. She sent her children to school, saved her money under a mattress, counted the coins from the jukeboxes, and paid the people who flipped burgers behind the counter a fair wage.

Back then, the newly arriving Greeks, with their swarthy complexions and sturdy builds, were considered not merely interloping foreigners but also biological inferiors: lazy, dirty, uncivilized, untrustworthy, no matter how diligently they applied themselves to the tasks of productivity and of fitting in. "A large per cent. of immigration," wrote the journalist Frank Julian Warne in 1916, "is made up of outcasts, criminals, anarchists, thieves, and offscourings of the earth, who are forced to leave their own lands and still are allowed to land upon American soil. Isn't it time we begin to take measures to stop this inflow of foreign scum?"

It was a matter of politics but also of race—that human invention which, like borders, is a fiction that carries the gravest consequences. "I have seen gatherings of the foreign-born in which narrow and sloping foreheads were the rule," wrote the American sociologist E. A. Ross in his book *The Old World in the New*—published in 1914, the year my great-grandmother touched land. "Among the women, beauty . . . was quite lacking. . . . There were so many sugar-loaf heads, moon-faces, slit mouths, lantern-jaws, and goose-bill noses that one might imagine a malicious jinn had amused himself by casting human beings in a set of skew-molds discarded by the Creator," he continued. "That the Mediterranean peoples are morally below the races of northern Europe is as certain as any social fact."

In 1909, an Irish police officer in Omaha arrested a Greek man for vagrancy—studying English alone with a white woman. On their way to the jailhouse, the Greek man pulled out a gun and killed the cop. "The blood of an American is on the hands of these Greeks," a prominent Nebraska attorney announced, blaming the community for the act of a single man. The shooter's life had been too easy in the Land of the Free, according to an article in the *Omaha World-Herald*. "He was made to feel that he was a human being. He grew fat in arrogance and pushed aside the native sons or used them as mere rungs of his ladder of success."

People longer settled in Omaha distrusted these foreigners, and the shooting was the last straw. A mob set forth on south Omaha, where roughly twelve hundred Greeks lived, working mostly in the nearby meatpacking plants and on the railroads. The mob ravaged the neighborhood, smashing the windows of the Greeks' shops and homes with bricks. (Some turned on Romanians and Turks, too, unable to tell the difference.) The mob gave the immigrants twenty-four hours to leave town if they wanted to stay alive. Omaha was thus emptied of its Greeks.

Like most everything else in the United States, this racial caste system was likely somewhat confounding to my great-grandmother when she arrived. But her skin was light enough; in spite of her dark eyes and olive skin (my inheritance), if she dressed right and stayed out of the sun and concealed her rough accent, she could pass. Eventually along with other southern Europeans, Greek Americans came to be considered white, as if by some hidden, silent consensus. There were other newcomers, by then, on whom to turn the bricks.

Whether or not my great-grandmother considered herself white from the outset, or used her appearance for both assimilation and ascension, I don't know. She raised her kids to resemble true US Americans, though at home they spoke Greek out of earshot of others. In the summer, when her daughters turned too tan after taking the bus to Connecticut's beaches, she scolded them. And in her later years, she talked about the new people moving into her New Haven neighborhood, where she herself had once been considered a stranger—"them," and "too many" of them. She meant Black people. This country had taught Evanthia its hierarchy, and she had assimilated and internalized that mythology in full.

9.

A century after my family's arrival in the United States, Moria camp caught fire and the six young Afghans were arrested. I knew that an even harsher, less porous version of the hierarchy of belonging that my relatives encountered had forged Moria: that tinderbox of a camp, that effective prison. And I knew immediately that I wanted to speak with the Moria 6 to hear their side of the story.

I tried to visit them in prison and to contact them via email, but the authorities denied each of these attempts. Eventually I wrote the defendants a letter that their lawyers delivered to them. Ali wrote me back and told me his version of things.

After their arrests, he explained, the six of them were arraigned in Mytilene, loaded onto an Athens-bound ferry, and driven to a prison on the outskirts of the city. From the window of the vehicle, Ali watched the European mainland moving past. This wasn't the arrival in Athens he'd pictured: papers in hand and walking free. He'd mostly relinquished his optimism by now. The six of them would have their day in court, but Ali already sensed that it didn't matter to the Greek authorities whether he'd committed the crime or not. Once they were arrested, their fates were written. Ali had lived in Greece long enough to understand that the image Europe projected to the world—a place of strength, where freedom and justice prospered—was, at least for refugees like him, a sham. He could hold out hope, because hope was all he really had, but optimism was a different story. If he and the others were found guilty, they'd serve their time and then would likely be deported back to Afghanistan, with nothing to show for the thousands of dollars they'd spent to get to Greece and the years of freedom they'd lost.

As the trials neared, the government persisted with its version of things: A group of angry young refugees had lit the fire. But as I went deeper into the reporting, I couldn't find any real evidence that the Moria 6 were guilty, or had any motive. Why would Ali, with his long-awaited asylum interview scheduled so soon, have lit the fire? One of the other young men was scheduled to be officially reunited with his brother in France in a matter of months. Why would he have jeopardized that chance?

The government presented its case against the Moria 6 as a clear-cut, cause-and-effect sequence: these boys were furious over their fates as refugees stuck inside Moria for so long, and they lit the fire in a fit of rage. A linear story is often the simplest to tell, but it is generally made linear only as a result of key omissions or oversimplifications. In the case of the Moria fire, the government's story just didn't add up. With the slightest prodding, it seemed to fracture then fall apart.

At the school where I worked as an administrator for many years, teachers teach sequencing language—words like *first, next, later, finally, last*—so that students can assign an order to their sentences and ideas. *First* the teachers teach the sequencing words, *then* they teach the students how to string them together to create an arc, a line through time.

Students at the high school are recently arrived immigrants who are learning English. They've come to the United States from all over the world. It's hard to learn a new language, particularly if fear and shame are involved—fear of what this new and unforgiving country might hold in store, shame for not having the words in the dominant language to say what you need or what you mean. While we all learn differently, there is a common arc to language learning: *First* we listen, absorbing what's around us. *Then* we begin to understand what's being said. *Eventually* we begin to form words on our own, and *following that* is when we learn to read and *subsequently* to write—since it's difficult to form words on a page *before* we know what they mean in the world.

Basic sequencing language insists on order and presumes a world where things unfold in a straight line. More advanced sequencing language, however, which at the school tends to be taught in later years, includes words like *previously, meanwhile, since, prior to that.* These are words that transcend the determined march in a single direction; they allow for lateral movement, for circling back in time, for simultaneous occurrence. The more advanced sequencing words acknowledge that life doesn't happen in neat arcs or ordered epiphanies, and that not every story can be formulated in tidy succession.

Back when my great-grandmother arrived in the United States, European immigrants, after enduring the indignities of Ellis Island and the xenophobia that spread through their new country like a strangling vine, generally had the chance to apply for citizenship. Compared with what it takes to become a citizen now—English proficiency, years of waiting, astronomical application fees, elaborate background checks, memorizing a hundred questions in order to pass an in-person test—Evanthia's process was easy. In 1929, fifteen years after she arrived and by which time she had given birth to four American children, she filled out some paperwork and was sworn in as a citizen. Her proximity to whiteness, and her family's eventual inclusion within that category, was her shelter.

She had passed through Ellis Island because the 1891 Immigration Act had established the place as an official port of entry into the United States. The island was part processing center, part prison—no border wall needed, for, like Lesbos, it was surrounded by water. This was the first detention center built explicitly for immigrants in the known history of the world. (The second, Angel Island, would open in 1910 in the San Francisco Bay for people crossing from the other side of the globe.)

By the time Evanthia naturalized, as the term goes, in 1929, it had gotten harder for people like her to make it into the country in the first place. In 1921, capitalizing on post–World War I unease, the federal government launched the Emergency Quota Law, limiting how many people from various countries would be admitted and thus severely restricting the number of immigrants coming from anywhere other than western Europe. Then Congress passed the Immigration Act of 1924, more popularly known as the Johnson-Reed Act, to further curb immigration and "preserve U.S. homogeneity," a government historian would later write. The act instituted a quota system limiting arrivals to the United States based on population numbers from the 1890 census, when the vast majority of residents were from northern and western Europe, and expanded the way the quota categories were calculated, thus further favoring immigration from those countries. After the Johnson-Reed Act, only around one hundred Greeks would be allowed in per year; people from Africa, Asia, and the Arabic-speaking world had almost no pathways to entry. Border fortification takes many forms, including laws.

But even the story of immigration exclusions doesn't move in a straight line. After World War II, international refugee law was born, acknowledging the humanitarian responsibility to protect those persecuted out of their homelands. The eleven original signatories to the 1951 Convention Relating to the Status of Refugees—mostly European countries—defined who could be considered a refugee and agreed to offer shelter and legal protection to those who had been uprooted by persecution during World War II; in 1967, the definition of a refugee was expanded to cover anyone fleeing because of a well-founded fear of persecution based on race, religion, political opinions, nationality, or membership in a particular social group. (Today, there are 149 signatories to the 1951 convention and its 1967 expansion.) In 1965, as the civil rights movement gained momentum, the US government eliminated the long-standing race-based admission quotas and began prioritizing visas for family reunification and "skilled labor." Over the next thirty years, more than 13 million people from around the world, including nearly 200,000 Greeks, would immigrate to the United States as a result of these new pathways. In 1980, with millions of people displaced in Southeast Asia (largely as a result of US military action), Jimmy Carter signed the Refugee Act into law with tremendous bipartisan support. The Refugee Act of 1980 essentially codified international refugee law, which we call asylum, into US immigration law. It also formalized our national resettlement program, establishing an annual quota of refugees to be resettled to the United States each year from overseas. Offering refuge was now an institutionalized form of humanitarian relief.

When Ronald Reagan took office as president, he made immigration restrictions a priority yet again—in part in reaction to the liberal expansion of refugee policy in the previous administration. By then, the

United States had been incarcerating immigrants for nearly a century, but the Reagan administration launched the first detention quota, ensuring that at any given moment a minimum of 10,000 immigrants would be locked up. But where would they be housed? This political landscape was fertile ground for immigration profiteering. In 1983, the Corrections Corporation of America (now CoreCivic) became the world's first major private prison company, reaping profit from public dollars to detain people in both the immigration and the criminal justice systems. The more people were locked up, and the longer they were locked up for, the more money such a company stood to make.

By the time Barack Obama took the presidency, an average of 33,400 immigrants were being held in US detention facilities each day, roughly 70 percent of them in facilities run by private companies turning a profit on their imprisonment. The Obama administration deported more immigrants per year than ever before—more, even, than the Trump administration would. When Donald Trump was elected, the stocks of private prison companies soared. It was a good bet. His administration built more than twenty new detention facilities and kept people locked up for longer periods of time. During his term in office, roughly 50,000 immigrants were in detention on an average day.

As in Greece, the US asylum process can take a long time, even years. The law allows for asylum seekers to be provisionally released pending their asylum decision so long as they are not deemed a flight risk or a threat to society (according to court standards, the vast majority of asylum seekers are not). But under Trump, this policy was largely ignored. People seeking protection in the United States would do so from inside a prison, sometimes waiting for years.

In the United States, as in Greece, winning asylum isn't easy, even for those with a strong case. The process places a tremendous burden of proof on the appellant to demonstrate not just the fact of their persecution but the extent of it, and that their home country is unable or unwilling to protect them. Securing such proof can be difficult. How can you prove that you got the scar on your face at the hands of a gang rather than in some kind of farm accident? When you didn't report it to the police because the police were protected by the gangs, or vice versa, or because you feared further reprisal? How could you prove that the army officer beat you so badly you could no longer properly breathe? That your family would murder you for being gay? That the Taliban would murder you for having worked for the Americans? You need photographs. Witnesses. Police reports. Expert testimony. And you need to assemble your story of persecution into a neat, sequenced timeline. *First, next, after that, after that, and then, and then, and then.*

More than a third of the students at the high school where I work are applying for some kind of immigration relief here in the United States and thus must learn to narrate the story of the threats against their lives in as much detail as possible. Any deviation, any faltering, any misplaced fact risks the applicants' being disbelieved and their applications' being rejected—and thus being deported back to the very danger they were trying to flee. The legal process assumes, and even requires, that memory is infallible, and that we recall things in perfect order.

No brain remembers everything exactly as it happened, but a brain that has experienced trauma has even more difficulty doing so. Trauma can fundamentally alter brain chemistry, leading to a vast array of health problems, sleeplessness, a sense of hypervigilance even in times of calm, and impaired memory. How to remember, with exactitude, the most painful moments of your life? The very fact of trauma can work against a person seeking protection as a result of the events that caused it.

Asylum seekers also often find their claims rejected because their stories sound too alike. Yet it makes sense that the stories will resemble one another, like echoes. A repressive government will use standardized surveillance and torture tactics; an army will rape and pillage in familiar ways; a gang will enact similar rules, and similar punishments for breaking them. Horror can be highly regulated, deeply ordered. But to some judges and asylum officers, such similarities indicate fraud.

In fact, the longer that immigration judges and asylum officers work at their jobs, the higher their rejection rates. Hear enough miserable stories and a person can begin to shut down, become hardened. Mercy leaks away. One also becomes susceptible to vicarious trauma. A 2009 study found high rates of secondary traumatic stress among immigration judges. "I am concerned," expressed one of the study's scientists, "that the stress and trauma in judges may make it hard for them to recognize trauma in the refugees whose cases come before them in the courtroom." Disbelief becomes both a weapon and a shield.

Secondary trauma, remarkably, manifests the same way it does for someone who has experienced trauma firsthand; the brain doesn't differentiate. In this way, vicarious trauma is a rather stunning metaphor: what happens to any one of us can affect the rest.

Were my great-grandmother applying for asylum today, she would almost certainly be rejected. She wasn't fleeing danger, after all—poverty, lethal as it can be, is not considered a protectable category under either international refugee law or domestic US asylum policy.

But even if she qualified, her paperwork would raise some flags. On some documents it says she was born in Athens, but her birth certificate and the ship's manifest state clearly that she was born on Andros.

I don't know why my great-grandmother would have lied on her US papers about her biography—and perhaps it wasn't a lie at all, just a misunderstanding, or a shorthand for the sake of clarity, for who in the States had ever heard of Andros then? For all intents and purposes, Athens was Greece, and that's where she was from. But I do know that today, an immigrant who proffers such falsified information will have their application summarily rejected, the false information read as an attempt to defraud the US government. If someone lies once, the thinking goes, what else are they hiding?

I once read an opinion from an immigration judge in Texas denying an asylum claim. If he believed the applicant's story, he wrote, he would have granted the asylum, but he didn't believe her because she had crossed the border unauthorized, which only a dishonest person—someone who shouldn't be believed—would do. Here, the logic of sequence had been fashioned into a perfect circle, looping for eternity, a single continuous line.

When does an immigration story start? *First,* my great-great-grandfather left home. *Then* my great-grandmother sailed the seas to join him. But what had happened *prior to that* to cause him to go? And what was his daughter's life like *in the meantime*? And what of all the other lives—

Ali's journey, for instance, and the millions of others who'd left their homes, Europe-bound, and found themselves stuck in Greece, a place with its own instability? Nothing ever happens "first," because a million things have always happened before. We don't live steadily toward epiphany; our truest stories move back and forth in time, in space, in memory. Life is a mosaic, not a line.

10.

Though each of my trips to Greece was structured around a quest for information, as was not the case on other reporting ventures, I was intentionally veering off path. I felt the need to move through the map of the country to better understand the contemporary refugee crisis and my own family's origin story, and to study the mythologies that shaped both. Yet to find my way through the questions I had set out to unravel seemed also to require entering uncharted spaces. As with our misadventure on Hydra, these expeditions gave way to encounters that verged on the magical, the mystic.

For instance: One morning, Ben and I meandered through Athens's quiet alleyways until, as if toppling from another dimension, we arrived at Metropolis Square. Suddenly we were surrounded by throngs of people navigating a congested outdoor mall: an H&M, a TOMS shoe store, a wine bar, a place selling upscale fur.

We moved through the crowds until we were standing in front of a Byzantine church. The building was cathedral-like in design but tiny, as if it had been miniaturized and glued to the cobbles of the square. The frenzy of commerce, combined with the elegance of the building and its strangeness of scale, gave the shrunken cathedral the feeling of an apparition, or something from a dream. We circled it slowly, admiring its walls made of crude marble, the smooth archways and crisscrossing brickwork that laced across the cupola, while everyone else around us hurried past.

We sat on a shady ledge on the church's northern edge, sweat cooling our shoulders. I noticed some activity in front of me and looked up. There, standing on a stone bench just a few feet away, was a handsome duck who was positively squawking at a striking stiff-backed woman with long auburn hair.

At first the duck, with his sleek coat of green, seemed to be an escapee of some nearby pond or fountain, but we soon realized that the woman and the duck were a pair. Not only was the duck berating her, but she was speaking back. He would quack her way and she would in turn admonish him in Greek in a tone of severity that also had a touch of tenderness, like that of a strict mother or an exasperated wife. Like this, they were engaged in an emphatic interspecies conversation—one that, to judge from both the ire and the aura of familiarity (*This again!*) with which the duck quacked and the woman retorted, seemed to have been going on for quite some time, maybe even for centuries. Ben and I looked at each other in disbelief.

The long-haired woman rummaged in her tote, pulled out a small plastic container, and pried open the lid. She set it down and the duck began to eat from it happily. This silenced him for a while, but the moment he finished he was quacking again. I would have felt sorry for the woman if she hadn't seemed so self-possessed, so unruffled by it all. She pulled out another container—this one filled with water—and set it down next to the first. The duck dipped his beak with delight, lapping and splashing about like a happy child. Once he'd finished, he resumed his reproach, and she hers, and like that we sat for many minutes on the ledge by the Byzantine church, watching a duck squabble with his austere human mother.

It felt fair to wonder whether we'd slid through an invisible slit in the daylight and into some extraordinary realm, as if we'd conjured one of the Greek myths or one of Ovid's tales of metamorphosis, this scenario not unlike that of a pleading daughter transformed into a tree, Odysseus's soldiers changed into pigs, a self-obsessed boy consigned to living as a flower, forever peering downward at its own reflection. These references were nearly impossible to escape in a US education, which was steeped in them—plus, I had to admit, I liked the stories. But here, it seemed, was an uncanny transfiguration right in front of me, no longer confined to the page. During these visits to Greece, every moment seemed like it could so easily shape-shift into something else entirely; the smallest things felt touched with meaning, riddles that meant more than met the eye. Or maybe the magic was of my own conjuring—myths I myself was willing into being.

What was this little chapel, anyway? I consulted the map on my phone. It was called the Little Metropolis Church, and it had been built in the Byzantine style, likely around the thirteenth century—an epoch in Greece many history books gloss over or ignore, Beaton suggests, as it muddies the connection between Acropolis-era ancients and modern-day Greeks. There are also theories that the church was built under the Ottomans, as a place of Orthodox worship when the Ottomans were converting many existing places of worship into mosques. Its date of origin is difficult to establish because it was fashioned out of materials repurposed from buildings that once stood elsewhere in the city. What is certain is that the place where it stands was once the site of a temple to Eileithyia, the goddess of midwifery and childbirth. Before Christianity, women had come here, just as they had to the spring on the quiet, poppy-strewn edge of the Acropolis, to leave offerings in the hope for a child.

Nearly everything begins as something else. Athens, for example, has been many cities, each constructing itself around and atop the last. "There is no ideal ensemble of the past buried underneath the contemporary city, only infinite fragments," argues Svetlana Boym. She is examining the way nostalgia works within and upon an urban landscape—its construction and renovations, its memorials and belief centers, how its visitors and inhabitants narrate the story of the city and how it came to be. What is built and preserved and rebuilt is a reflection of what the architects want to believe—or what they want others to believe—about history. "The ruin is not merely something that reminds us of the past," she writes. "It is also a reminder of the future, when our present becomes history." We're just a layer of paint on the walls of a many-centuries-old house.

Ben and I turned to confer with each other, and by the time we spun back around, the duck and his mother were gone.

11.

These bizarre moments piled up. Were they curses, benedictions? The encounters bewildered me, and they bewitched me, too. They gave me the impression of having trespassed into a mythic world. It began to dawn on me that perhaps these eerie occurrences weren't detours from the work I had come to do but clues or some kind of key to it. It was as if I was assembling my own canon of myths that echoed with the themes of estrangement and belonging I had traveled to Greece to parse. For myths, as the classicist Peter Struck puts it, are a kind of cultural DNA narrating "the story of where you are from." Across traditions, these stories are teeming with heroes and monsters and transformations and epic trials, but also with autochthonous birth: a human being born from the land itself. In myth, beings are forever bound to an original homeland. But not always so in life. Try as we might to conjure direct lineage from a singular motherland, my family—and so many families on this earth—is descended from generations of movement, of wandering or uprooting, by choice or by force.

A few years ago, without informing us of his plans, my brother spit into a tube to have his DNA tested, only to learn that our oldest ancestors weren't, in fact, Greek—not necessarily, and not in any original or particular way. "Greece" didn't show up at all on the test. Genetically speaking, it turns out, the Greek side of our family is Italian and

"Balkan"—from somewhere within that broad designation, of which Greece is only sometimes listed as part. Greece, then, is only a single leg of a long ancestral journey, one still underway.

"I don't believe it," my aunt replied to the news on the family email chain.

"The test is wrong," my dad agreed. "We're Greek!" *The story of where you are from.*

Once I attended with my poet friend Camille a reading of poems inspired by classical myths. The hour dragged, we grew bored. The tales seemed inert—homages to the original rather than reinvigorations. "Is it okay for a poet to be aggressively uninterested in Greek mythology?" Camille tweeted as we exited the theater.

Over drinks after the reading, we discussed the fundamentally exclusive nature of an established canon and the way classical mythology was worn from overuse, from having been so often rewritten and referenced and reimagined, and from having been shoved so far down the throats of college students, as though ingesting them was some sort of entry requirement to being taken seriously. But I also had to admit to her that the book I was writing was fat with Greek mythology and reference to classical ideas.

"That's different," she said. "It's your heritage."

The problem with my diasporic condition, though, one I share with many white people in the United States, is that it can feel as if my roots carry information critical to my identity—and at the same time, because I have no concrete, lived connection with Greece, as if I wear my heritage like a costume.

I already harbored hesitations about the "Greece book," as I'd come to call it. It would be absurd and inhumane, I knew, to attempt any comparison between my own family's story and that of today's refugees. Yet there was an undeniable connection between my desire to belong to this long-lost homeland and the fact and function of contemporary borders.

White US Americans often pursue and cling to a pre-American heritage in order to feel part of something more meaningful than, well, US American whiteness. Ancestry services like 23andMe have seen a boom in recent years, in spite of the controversy surrounding them (what they are allowed to do with our DNA data, for instance, and whether the results are even all that accurate). People want proof of where they've come from, of *who they really are.* It's not just white US Americans who, cleaved by migration, crave an origin story; others, having been stripped of their histories via enslavement, gaps in the archive, adoption, and family silences, seek this information, too. And is it so surprising that so many of us yearn for a root system to tether us? That we hurtle toward an identity deeper and more complex than daily life in a globalized, capital-driven world often allows? The hunger for belonging is perhaps best understood as an attempt to rewrite the ancient myths—those tales that explained the birth of the world and our place within it. The desire for an origin story might seem innocent enough if it weren't so often yoked to the impulses to rank, to dominate, and to exclude.

I remember my great-grandmother Evanthia as a wiry, ardent ram of a woman with a broad smile, thick-rimmed black glasses, and stiff, dowdy old-world clothing: smocklike skirts, stockings that bunched and bagged at her ankles. She spoke some English but not all that much. But I knew her as my matriarch, and I loved her for that, and for the way she was. She had come from far, far away, and she had made for us a home. She loved us all back, her US American descendants. For she believed in us and in "America"—not the country, but the idea. It had worked for her.

It is an inherited truism in my family that, because of the determined grit of Evanthia, that teenage "domestic" who traveled here from faraway rocky shores, we all were able to become who we are. That alchemy of personal determination and the flashing promise of the USA—you could catch it, if you tried, and bottle it, like a firefly; how it throbbed with light. And hadn't she?

Then again, of her four children, only two managed to outlive her. Of Theodore, the World War II veteran, it was only said that it was the war that killed him. And maybe in a roundabout way that was true, but the technical, if hushed, fact is that he died because he took a gun and shot himself in the head. (Or perhaps, according to other family members, he took pills? The truth is buried with him; I'll never know. Orthodox burials are prohibited to suicides, but in any case, as part of their assimilation, the family had shifted to the Anglican church.) There is hardly anything of Theodore's life or death in the otherwise copious family archive of stories. Tula, my grandmother's more beautiful and vivacious sister, struggled with alcoholism and died a tragic, early death that left a gaping family wound.

My family doesn't dwell on the tragedies, the casualties of migration and war and loss and of grasping toward ascension. Instead we boast of our heritage and the path it took to get here, for we are (we are determined to believe) a success story. Any inside presupposes an outside; any insider, outsiders. My life is nothing if not proof that we're on the right side of the wall now. In the current world order, my belonging will always be at someone else's expense.

12.

Though no family on earth can claim a single fixed place of origin, I was nevertheless drawn to Andros, where Evanthia was born, as if it held crucial clues to who my family was and the circumstances that had forged us. One morning, from the Aegean port of Rafina, Ben and I boarded a passenger ferry to the island, where I'd booked us an Airbnb overlooking the sea.

The place where we'd be staying wasn't easy to find on the map, so our host, Pavlos, a lean man in his sixties with tight gray curls and bright, flashing eyes, met our ferry to show us the way. The route hooked north from the small port into the hills via dirt road after dirt road and even one road made of pure sand. We were to stay in the spare, light-filled apartment above Pavlos's house, which was built into the rocky hillside. Before we settled in, he insisted we join him for breakfast.

We came downstairs to a feast set out on the terrace overlooking the rocky coast: bread, tahini, a jar of honey, boiled eggs, coffee, milk, nuts, yogurt, and a few oranges—bold, glowing orbs he'd cut in two. The bread, baked with cinnamon and currants, was particularly delicious, and I said so. Pavlos explained that his brother had brought it as a gift from a recent visit to Cyprus, where his family was originally from. He and his brother and sister had been raised in a small town, in a house surrounded by orange groves. In Cyprus, he explained, Greeks and Turks had long lived together more or less peaceably—under the Ottomans, as a British colony, and then as an independent state. But when Pavlos was in his twenties, that changed. Stoked, in part, by the long-running animosity between the Greek and Turkish states, violence erupted in Pavlos's home, dividing the island in two: Turks to the north, Greeks to the south. During the war, many Greek Cypriots like Pavlos's family were forced to flee.

We listened to his story and continued to eat our breakfast, spreading tahini over the bread, peeling the eggs. The wind picked up suddenly and we hurried to secure our napkins with our forks, tuck the eggshells into empty coffee cups. Pavlos had been in Athens studying, he recounted, when things in Cyprus really took a turn. He had managed to bring his brother, his sister, and his parents to join him in safety. They never lived in Cyprus again.

"War. That's how it is, this is how things happen."

Now the wind whipped up into a true howl, but Pavlos seemed either not to notice or not to care. The coffee cups tipped and eggshells scattered off the table, napkins took flight. He kept on with his story. Years after the war had ended and it was safe to return, Pavlos decided to see what was left of their home. The house was still there but it was practically unrecognizable. The orange groves had been razed.

"Gone," he said. He took an orange off the table and held it in his fist. "You cannot believe what these people have done. The most beautiful trees, can you imagine? Nothing, nothing. Gone." When he returned from his trip, he fell sick with fever for many days. Losing your home like that, he said, will make a person ill.

Pavlos wanted to show us the area, including a small beach nearby, so that evening we took a walk eastward on the lonely road. He pointed out the many wildflowers, the spectacular view across the sea toward the mainland. Nearly all the houses we passed were empty, with a withered grandeur; time and the elements were wresting them from human grip. Here a swimming pool was filled with dirt and leaves, there the paint was cracking and eroding, the windows shattered, the small statue at the front door toppled, the gates unhinged, the gardens reverted to weeds or just sun-cracked earth.

We peered over the walls of these compounds so Pavlos could assess the latest decay and tell us who had built the house, who had recently bought it, where these owners now lived, many of them once but no longer rich because, as we knew, *what has happened in this country.* "These people do not take care of this house," he said of one, and of another, "These people sold to a very rich man, but he never comes."

Pavlos was a grandfather now, and a formerly retired dentist. Because his pension had been cut, he'd had to go back to work. His kids didn't visit the house on Andros much anymore, for it was costly to get there, and they had their own lives, their own livelihoods to earn. He himself could go back and forth only so much, given the price of a ferry ticket. The house was a great expense; there was no water on that edge of the island, so he had to truck it in and store it in large tanks, and the costs increased every year. Though it was difficult to make a living as an older man, he was optimistic. He pointed out a development of small, unfinished houses up on the hillside, stalled by the economic collapse. Something, someday, would turn things around.

We scrambled down the path to the small beach, which was empty. From the clear waters—"Paradise!" Pavlos announced—the skeletons of half-built houses on the hillside above us, gilded by the waning sun, appeared majestic rather than forlorn. Pavlos smiled as he swam, taking us so far out around a rocky protrusion of the island that I struggled to keep my breath.

That night, the wind wailed so monstrously about Pavlos's home that we could hardly sleep, even though we were dead tired. I was certain it would quell by morning. But in the morning, there was Pavlos at our door with coffees, the wind making a mess of his hair and clothing. "Beautiful day!" he told us as the apartment whistled and shook. "Not so windy today. Today will be very good." He asked if we would like to go for a hike with him so he could show us the island's stunning and intricate loops of trails. We had hoped to spend the day just the two of us, but it was a kind offer, and he seemed to long for company, so we agreed. "It is not good to be in paradise alone," he had practically whispered to Ben through the wind the day before.

Now Pavlos opened the map to show us where our hike would take us.

"Where did your great-grandmother live on this island?" Pavlos asked me, but I had no idea. It was disappointing to us both. It was only from my brother's DNA test that I'd learned she was not from Athens but from Andros. And it was too bad, Pavlos noted, that my family hadn't taught me to speak Greek. With this, too, I agreed.

He slapped the map. "Here is good," he said, sweeping his hand over the central quadrant of the island, "and also here and down here. But here," he added, hovering his open palm over the northern third, "there is nothing. Nothing! You do not go here. Okay?" It felt like some kind of warning.

We loaded into our rental car, crossed the island, and hiked all day in the sunshine, taking small pathways that looped among quiet houses and rushing springs. There were wild plums we could pluck straight off the branches on the hillside, apricot trees and mulberries, the perfect assortment of sun and shade. On this side of the island there was far less wind, and wherever we were in the presence of running water—water so clean and clear you could drink it—we felt at ease. I tried to imagine my great-grandmother on these paths as a girl, but could only ever picture her as an old woman.

Our trail lowered us down a hillside along a creek, which we'd follow until eventually we'd find a beach. After walking for a while, we came to a narrow pasture where a donkey stood as if waiting for us, calling out to us with its eyes, we felt, to come near. "This donkey loves people," Pavlos told us. As Ben stroked the soft space between its eyes and down along its muzzle, the donkey was practically purring. But soon the creature stiffened, locked eyes with him, bared its teeth, and bit into Ben's arm, hard. Ben twisted and pulled, but, as if possessed, the donkey wouldn't let him loose. When Ben finally managed to break free, his arm now bruised with a ring of deep purple, the donkey continued to reach for him and bray for his return. "Ha, this donkey, it really loves people!" Pavlos said again as Ben fingered the welt on his arm. He bid us to continue down the path along the donkey's narrow pasture. But the creature followed us as we accelerated to a sprint, calling for attention with brays so desperate they sounded like a woman's anguished screams.

This donkey had seemed possessed, human, as if begging us for something or beckoning us into another realm. Ben had seen it, too, hadn't he? Again our eyes met, as they had witnessing the woman and her duck. Ben was as spooked as I was. What on earth was going on?

We walked for a while longer in silence until we came to another small clearing, piled with dry tangles of brush. Ben pointed down into a bramble patch where two snakes coiled against each other, their bodies twisting so tightly that they moved in a propulsive, gravity-defying upward coil: liquid, muscular, like an ancient, ecstatic ballet. "Maybe they are in love," said Pavlos as the snakes spun, lifting and then falling back into the brush, lifting and falling. It was hard to tell if one was in pursuit and the other attempting to get away, or both attempting to pursue or both attempting to flee. Their grammar was completely foreign to us, and utterly magnetic. The bewitched donkey, these twirling snakes, felt like missives to decode, but here I was again, grasping at meaning and situating myself right smack in the center of the map.

Back on our side of the island that night, it seemed as though the wind might dislodge our apartment from the top of Pavlos's house and lift us away. I had a headache; Ben was uncharacteristically jittery and unmoored. An eerie feeling crowded the house, some presence of unwelcome. We felt shaken, and it was hard to fall asleep. Between the wind, the lack of water, the tumbledown houses, and the road that practically disappeared each day under the sand, it was clear to us that no one was meant to live on these particular cliffs. *Do not go here.* But Pavlos had fought so hard for his tiny empire. *It's no good to be alone in paradise.* He wanted us to love it as he did.

It occurred to me that Pavlos and I were mirrors of each other: me, determined to return to a homeland I'd never had, and him determined to re-create a home he'd lost. "Nostalgia is an ache of temporal distance and displacement," writes Svetlana Boym. "Displacement is cured by a return home, preferably a collective one. Never mind if it's not your home; by the time you reach it, you will already have forgotten the difference."

Over the next few days, we continued to feel an overwhelming sense—not from Pavlos, but from some other force—that we were unwelcome there. We didn't want to hurt his feelings by abandoning his paradise, but eventually we knew we had to go. The morning he was set to travel back to Athens, we snuck out, leaving the small offering of flowers and an apricot we'd set out the night before to appease the wind and whatever presence seemed to be demanding our departure.

We decided to catch the ferry to Mykonos, the partygoers' paradise just a few islands south, and try our luck there. There we found an unease of an entirely different, man-made kind. Gigantic cruise ships crowded the port, and we could barely walk from one side of the town to another, so crammed was it with people who'd spent too much time drinking in the sun. The island was flat but, like Andros, also terribly windy; amid the luxury hotels and fancy shops sand blew every which way. The abundance of spirit on Andros, eerie though it was, was nowhere to be found here; commerce had crowded it out. How easily a beautiful place could curdle with capital and human hunger.

So we returned to Andros, where we rented a room at a small inn in the main town on the island's eastern side. The wind blew softly there, and spring water tumbled down the mountainsides and emptied into the sea where we bobbed and read books, grateful for the rest and the quiet, for the welcome of an ecosystem that was, for now, intact. The town itself was quiet and carefree; everyone here (for now) still had a home. From time to time, military planes passed above us, but headed where and on what mission we couldn't know. And in truth we slept soundly, even amid the planes.

There was a road on Andros that veered into a protected, wind-free inner valley scattered with wildflowers. In the heat, we drove with the windows open, and occasionally a miraculous fragrance would sweep through the car—the kind of sweet, floral aromatic for which a perfumer would spend a lifetime in pursuit. When it was especially strong and the road was empty, we'd pull over to see if we could sniff out the source. It must, we thought, be the yellow flowers that painted the scrubland drifts. But each time we bent our noses to the blossoms we smelled nothing. The aroma tempted us like a siren's call yet was at once there and not there, and after a time I stopped pulling over, just kept my hands on the steering wheel and drove on.

The day we'd gone hiking with Pavlos, he'd taken us to the grocery store, where we ran into a younger couple who lived nearby. This couple often joined Pavlos for boat rides; they had picnics together, swam, enjoyed their shared heaven.

"You know," I'd overheard him saying forlornly in the pasta aisle, "I'm thinking of selling our house."

"Oh, no!" said the woman. "You can't sell! We'd miss you too much!"

"There's just no other way," said Pavlos. The finances, he said, just didn't add up.

"I didn't realize you were thinking of selling the house," I'd said when we were back in the car. From Pavlos's frown, I immediately understood that it wasn't a conversation I'd been meant to overhear.

"No, no," he said, shaking off the very notion. "This is my home. I can never leave this place."

13.

I'd fallen into journalism somewhat unexpectedly in my mid-twenties, wanting to write about things that I felt mattered most: migration, injustice, climate change, inequality. I loved the process of talking to people about their lives and how they saw the world, and then trying to meaningfully render onto the page what I had learned.

But over time I came to realize that, regardless of what I found during the process of reporting, editors often expected me to tell the story I'd been assigned in a particular, predetermined way, strung together in a straight line. And at the same time, I often found that the most moving things people told me, and the most stunning moments I observed—a little boy quietly celebrating his seventh birthday in a migrant shelter, the menacing sound of car keys jangling outside a motel room on a man's first night out on parole—fell outside the storyline I'd been assigned. If these details made it in at all, it was as sentimental asides. The more news-focused the outlets I wrote for became, the more often such moments were excised from my drafts. My job, it seemed, was to deliver the ordered arc.

As such, many of the pieces I wrote, and especially those related to immigration, began to resemble one another and the thousands of other stories just like them: stories that flattened people into characters, that built to a false epiphany and claimed some kind of "first."

. . .

Once, I went to southern Mexico to report a story about people from sub-Saharan Africa and South Asia who, "to avoid the clog of Europe," as I put it in my pitch, traveled to South America as a way of reaching the United States, overland.

This journey required crossing many borders, mostly on foot, to evade detection. The Mexican government referred to the overland crossers as "extra-continental migrants," or just "extra-continentals," since they hailed from continents other than the Americas. No matter where they came from, and without being asked, the dozens and dozens of people I spoke with would list the countries through which they'd passed in an almost trancelike incantation: *Brazil to Peru, Peru to Ecuador, Ecuador to Colombia, Colombia to Panama, Panama to Costa Rica, Costa Rica to Nicaragua, Nicaragua to Honduras, Honduras to Guatemala, Guatemala to Mexico.* Next stop: USA.

I spent most of my reporting time in Tapachula, a small city about forty miles north of the Guatemalan border. Here, transcontinental migrants slept in cheap hotels along Avenida Siete and frequented travel agencies specializing in domestic flights that allowed them to transit swiftly from Mexico's southernmost point to its north, near the US border. I learned quickly that these travelers often ate at a handful of restaurants on Seventh Avenue that offered non-Mexican fare, the most popular of which was Sadek's.

Sadek was originally from Bangladesh. He had landed several years earlier in Brazil, US-bound, but once he arrived in Tapachula, his cousin in the States stopped taking his calls. Sadek couldn't go home, but he couldn't easily press forward, so he decided to stay in Mexico. To make money, he opened a restaurant for what he knew was a growing clientele: passers-through, like him, from far away. He had no idea how to cook, but each night he'd call his sister in Bangladesh and she would talk him through the making of another dish. Eventually he rented an empty storefront, hired a few local women, and taught them to cook his sister's recipes.

He found another source of income, too. The overland journey from South America to the United States was so expensive that, by the time they ended up in Mexico, most migrants were deep in debt and strapped for cash. Sadek sometimes loaned people money, which he kept track of in a spiral-bound notebook. From where they started, these migrants could have traveled to Europe at roughly half what it cost them to get to the United States, but after 2015, they knew the odds: going that route, a person was likely to get stranded in some Greek island camp or Italian prison for years, if they even made it that far.

"People are dying in Sinai, they are becoming slaves in Libya, they drown in the Mediterranean," a man from Eritrea told me.

"In Europe, they don't give us papers," a man from Nigeria said. His cousins had, years before, managed to get visas in the UK, but for him, he felt, there'd be no hope.

"You go where you have the chance," a man from Gambia told me.

Crossing the Americas as these visa-less overlanders did required long treks on foot, bus and boat rides, sleeping on streets and in the forest, and occasionally—especially once they reached Central America—spending weeks on end in detention camps before being released to the next country, only to be detained once again by the authorities there. Of all these cursed crossings, there was one place that most everyone agreed was the worst by far: the Darién Gap, the choked stretch of jungle between Colombia and Panama.

Because it is so little populated, the Darién Gap, in addition to being mountainous terrain dense with poisonous plants and difficult to navigate, is a drug-smuggling corridor. Here, people were attacked and robbed and beaten and sometimes murdered. Guides would abandon their groups in the disorienting landscape, where there was no food, no reliable water source, no clear sense of where to go next. Many lost their way, their faith, their minds, their lives.

There are two kinds of stories journalists write about refugees," Theo Alexellis, a representative of the United Nations High Commissioner for Refugees (UNHCR) in Lesbos, told me over coffee. "They are either terrorists and criminals, or sad, pitiful charity cases." So what were my questions for him, he wanted to know.

It's true that much left-leaning immigration journalism is formulaic: *Desperate person leaves home, seeks aid in a bleak and brutal world.* Little attention is paid to the migrant's life as it was lived before leaving—and almost none to the nonbrutal aspects of that life. Similarly, the narrative of the journey itself is punctuated by horror, with little room for humor or joy or the rest of the journeyer's vast interior world. For whose interior world isn't vast, and singular? In this kind of journalism, the writer and the reader tend to be cast in the role of saviors, and the "characters"—the people on the move—are largely rendered as victims, stripped of agency and selfhood. The process is a bit like leveling the multidimensional intricacies of the world onto the flat page of a map.

At times I've fiercely resisted these traps of convention, and at others I've fallen headlong into them. It's so much easier, after all, to write the kind of story that's already been written. When I grew tired of writing this kind of magazine piece, I wrote a book about a Salvadoran family I had gotten to know. I knew their story deserved many, many pages, so that as much attention could be paid to their triumphs, their inner worlds, and their delight as to their suffering, fear, and US-bound dreams. When I returned to reporting and to writing for magazines, I looked not just for new stories but also for new and rounder ways to tell them. I knew, too, that I'd eventually have to turn the mirror on my own family—to excavate the migrations and borders that have determined my life, to parse a larger global history of migration, and to experience a little of the great vulnerability I so often asked of others: to be rendered a character on the page.

One night at Sadek's, I met four young men from Pakistan. They sat at a table waiting for their food, their four phones plugged into the wall, four plastic bags tied in perfect knots at their feet. They'd just been released from Siglo XXI, or Century 21, the colossal, eerily named detention facility in Chiapas where they'd spent the past nine days. Their release paperwork decreed that they had twenty-one days to leave the country or they'd be locked up again and then sent home.

Muzammil had been a member of a separatist party back in Kashmir. He told me that after police threw rocks through his window and he received several death threats, he'd eventually moved to Senegal to live with his uncle. From there it wasn't difficult to find someone to help him arrange passage to Brazil. He borrowed money, paid a Pakistani man in Senegal, whom he referred to as his "agent," to sort out the logistics, and in 2017 boarded a plane. Including airfare, lodging, food, on-the-ground travel logistics, and smugglers' costs, along with the "agent" fee, he had already spent $14,000 by the time he reached Sadek's, money he would have to pay back one day.

See how a story can compress time like a vise, and how the journalist, like a puppeteer, chooses what matters—that is, what appears on the page?

In the resulting story, this paragraph appeared. It is what is called, in journalism, a "nut graf":

> The extra-continentals are the extreme outliers of a global migration crisis of enormous scale. Today, more than 65 million people around the world have been forced from their homes—a higher number than ever recorded, as people flee war, political upheaval, extreme poverty, natural disasters, and the impacts of climate change. Since 2014, nearly 2 million migrants have crossed into Europe by sea, typically landing in Italy or Greece. They hail from dozens of countries, but most are from Syria, Afghanistan, Iraq, and Nigeria—countries struggling with war, political repression, climate change, and endemic poverty. In the overall scope of migration, the numbers of extra-continentals are small—except when you consider how unlikely their journey, and just how far they've come.

A nut graf is a section early in a piece that, as journalist Chip Scanlan writes, "tells the reader what the writer is up to; it delivers a promise of the story's content and message." The nut graf tries to justify the story's telling and points readers in the direction the writer would like them to go.

Later in the piece, I wrote about how the foursome had been together since they met on the road in Colombia, in a small dusty town on the edge of the continent, as Muzammil had described it to me, looking over toward Panama, all of them in need of a guide. Muzammil, who spoke the best English, negotiated with a man who agreed to take them and about twenty other migrants from Pakistan through the Darién Gap to Panama. The man charged them each forty dollars. But once they were in the thick of the jungle—far enough in to be unable to retrace their steps out—he told everyone to take a seat and wait until he returned in a few minutes.

"We waited four or five hours," Muzammil recalled, "but he never came."

When the group realized that they'd likely been abandoned, they decided to keep going on their own. The walk was supposed to take just two days, and they each had in their backpacks only a few bottles of water and energy drinks, and some packets of biscuits. Their food ran out first, and then their water. They spent four days scrambling up steep hillsides and walking in circles, their shoes sodden, their feet blistered and swollen, their legs and arms cut up from the branches and thorns. Muzammil turned his ankle, fracturing his foot, but he kept walking. He couldn't afford to be frail—none of them could.

I could write this story only because Muzammil told it to me. As he did, under the fluorescent lights of Sadek's restaurant, his friend Sanaullah, who'd lived the journey alongside him, sat quietly at the table, earbuds in. Sanaullah wasn't interested, he told me, in revisiting the narrative of what had happened.

"I thought we would all die there," Muzammil continued. For eventually one of their friends lay down in the jungle and told the rest of the group to press on without him. He'd had enough: this was as far as he could go. Muzammil urged him to get up, telling him they must be close by now, that it wouldn't be much longer, that he simply had to keep moving. But his friend wouldn't budge. He had resigned himself to dying all alone in the middle of the Darién Gap, but Muzamil wouldn't accept this. He began screaming at his friend and then beating him with a stick to force him to keep going. The man yelped and moaned.

"I beat him so hard," Muzammil recalled to me, then fell quiet. He snatched his pack of cigarettes, muttered an "Excuse me," and went outside into the night.

Sanaullah looked at me with a shrug, then slid his phone across the table, offering me an earbud. A keening melody tore through the wires. "Religious music," he said, as we listened together under the restaurant's yellow-green lights. "To relax."

Eventually Muzammil came back inside. "I'm sorry," he said. "I'm a little bit drunk." He wiped his eyes. I returned the earbud to Sanaullah, who turned up the volume while Muzammil finished the story, catching me up to the present: this afternoon's release from detention, their plans to hop a flight to the US border in the coming days and cross.

How to write a story based on painful facts of another person's life is a complicated question rife with ethical hazard. It's not that rendering suffering is necessarily exploitative or reductive, but the more of these stories I published, the clearer it became that I had a mandate to not only allow another reality to live and thrive alongside the pain but also to let the protagonists determine the most important elements of their own stories.

I once heard the writer Aleksandar Hemon describe narrative—particularly for the exiled—as a space of sovereignty. You'd never know, for instance, of the difficulties of Muzammil's journey from his social media accounts. His Facebook page was all glamour shots in places new to him, selfies of well-dressed Muzammil in an airport, or in a city square, or on the bank of some great body of water—all invoking a sense of adventure, the persona of an entrepreneur with an intrepid streak, ready to chase luck and take on the world. "Nice," his friends from Pakistan commented. "Looking good, man."

And indeed, on Facebook, Muzammil wasn't a mere migrant, but a man in charge of how his tale was told. By the time he reached the US border, his loved ones didn't know he'd been locked up or robbed, or nearly starved. People travel with their stories—true and fabulist and everything in between—and the hope of more to come.

One night at Sadek's, Muzammil told me a story he'd heard in the Panamanian camps about a woman in the Darién Gap. Several of the other passers-through I'd spoken to had heard about her, too. She was from India, the people told me, and had been traveling overland through the Americas with her twelve-year-old daughter, US-bound. Because she was a woman, Muzammil explained—the vast majority of these migrants were men—and because she was heavyset, she simply couldn't make it through the relentless jungle on foot. After days of struggle, she sat down and refused to move, just as Muzammil's friend had done.

No one in her group, not even her daughter, could make her budge. After hours of pleading, they gave up. She sent her daughter with them, bidding them to make sure she made it safely to the United States. When they left, she lay down, waiting for death to take her.

But she didn't die. There alone in the jungle, the story goes, she regained her strength, scrounged something to eat, and survived. She learned the tricks and codes of the jungle, eventually making it her home. And she's still there, even now. She leaves food and water out for the migrants when she has it; sometimes, in turn, they leave it for her, or she'll pilfer it from their stashes as they sleep. Occasionally a group of pilgrims crosses her path and she tells them which direction to go. She doesn't retreat, she doesn't move ahead: she just stays put. This story, which Muzammil took as fact, seemed to comfort him. Somewhere in that punishing place lives a survivor, a maternal presence, a trickster, a patron saint: someone who has thwarted the journey itself, thoroughly changing the story.

From Tapachula, Muzammil took a plane to Tijuana, where he met up with a final guide to help him cross the border. *Difficult roads often lead to beautiful destinations.* This was his final post on his Facebook page before he scrambled into the United States, where he would, ultimately, be incarcerated for more than seven months, fighting for the right to stay and wondering whether, after everything he'd been through, he'd end up dying within those detention center walls.

He knew that thousands of miles south, where one continent met the other, more people were moving toward him through the jungle, legs cut up, feet soaked. And he believed that somewhere in that same jungle sat a woman who had turned a liminal space into a home, a terror into a shelter, a trap into a scrap of freedom. She watched over the extra-continentals as they moved north in their slow, bedraggled drift. What did it matter whether she was real or imagined? The tales we tell each other can serve as oracles, yes, and as medicine, too.

I think often of that woman in the Darién Gap, Muzammil's certainty of her existence. I can picture her as if I had made her acquaintance. I now wish the article I wrote had included her story. She was a testament to self-determination, to interiority and simultaneity and possibility, and to the way the mythic and magical populate what we understand to be matters of fact. But the editors cut it and I didn't protest.

14.

In late June 2019, two weeks into my first trip to Greece, I boarded an overnight ferry, sleeping alone in a small room nestled within the ship's dark bowels. I awoke early and went outside to watch the sun rise. The wind blew roughly. A dog stowed somewhere nearby barked and howled. I studied the horizon receding behind our wake, Greece to my right, Türkiye to my left, as we plowed northward through the slip of sea that separates the two countries, which once upon a time were not countries at all, just land where people lived. It's not flight but borders that make a refugee.

That year, like every year since I'd become a journalist, there were more forced migrants across the globe than ever before. But there was little news in the United States anymore of the enduring human rights abuses and hardships in Lesbos, or of the infamous Moria. Most US journalists kept the focus on our own borders and the spectacular human rights abuses occurring there—family separation, prolonged detention, medical neglect, mass deportation, forcing migrants to remain in Mexico while they fought their asylum cases in the United States.

The ship pulled into the east-facing harbor of Mytilene, where a friend awaited me. Thi Bui had been a founding teacher at the high school where I worked; she was also a writer and artist. Her own family had fled Vietnam by boat in 1978, spending time in a refugee camp in

Malaysia before resettling to the United States. A staunch advocate for migration rights, she, too, was in Lesbos doing research for a book.

From the harbor, Thi drove us straight to Moria.

Outside the main entrance to the camp, we met up with Morteza, a young man from Afghanistan who had lived in Moria for more than six months and who had agreed to be our interpreter. He was lean and tall—though he had the quality of appearing taller than he perhaps actually was. He stuck out his hand in greeting, then motioned to the Moria entrance. "Are you ready?" He led us forward with confidence and an air of dependability, at the same time giving the impression that at any instant something might call him elsewhere, causing him to vanish.

The camp was fortified with fencing and razor wire, like a prison, though at that point the authorities still allowed residents to come and go. People hung around the edges—families waiting for the bus, teens kicking a ball, women adjusting their headscarves while walking toward town beneath the relentless sun. *A camp becomes a city,* one of Ben's poems goes, *the way a wound becomes a scar.*

We showed our passports at the front gate and were waved inside, but a guard barked something to Morteza in Greek as he stepped across the threshold behind me. "He's with us," Thi said, and the guard shrugged, waving him in with a scowl. Inside, the UNHCR protection officer, Patric Mansour, began to lead us through Moria. Though the numbers were nothing like in 2015, he explained, arrivals were on the rise again, the camp having grown by nearly 2,000 people in the past few weeks alone. Now Moria was "home" to 5,300, making it the second-largest city on the island. That very morning, the occupants of two newly arrived boats were seated on the benches of the camp's welcome area waiting to be processed. The previous summer, Patric told us, there had been more than 9,000 people in Moria. "We didn't even have a place to put the garbage bins," he said.

Patric walked us through the camp, showing us the food stations where people picked up their daily rations, the small clinic, the welcome center, the enclosed areas where unaccompanied minors lived, the sagging tents and IsoBoxes where people set up their temporary lives. We moved through crowds of people idling or seeking an audience with Patric to lodge complaints. Children walked around with pieces of cardboard fastened to their heads like hats and made games of throwing rocks. Patric recounted how, in the winter, kids removed the doors from the IsoBoxes and slid down the icy hill. I'd visited many refugee and asylum-seeker settlements in the past—in Uganda, Kenya, Thailand, Mexico—and, as always, though perhaps more acutely this time, I felt like some kind of disaster tourist, my worst feelings about journalism throbbing beneath my skin.

Patric had worked in refugee settlements around the globe—in the Dadaab refugee complex in Kenya, where several hundred thousand people had sheltered and which was then the largest camp in the world, and later in Jordan, where the camps for Syrian refugees overtook even Dadaab in size. But the situation in Greece, he said, was more difficult than in any other place he'd worked. This was the EU and so, in theory, there were far more resources, but bureaucratic barriers and the stigma against refugees, both locally and regionally, hamstrung efforts to actually care for people.

"Here, even with funding, nothing is moving forward," he lamented. The previous year, he said, because of holdups to budget approvals he'd found himself having to raise money on his own just to purchase toilet paper for the camp.

Though almost all the people living in Moria who had their asylum approved were eligible for transfer, the process was slow—interminable, if you asked Morteza and his friends.

"It can take two weeks, it can take six months," Patric said. This was late June; it had been over a month since anyone was transferred to the mainland. With right-wing candidates from the New Democracy Party having taken power after recent elections, it would be at least another month, likely not until the fall, before any new transfers took place.

"It's bullshit. This is a disgrace," Patric said, looking out to the camp. People kept arriving, but no one was leaving. Not that the mainland necessarily offered much by way of opportunity, particularly in this country with a nearly 20 percent unemployment rate, pervasive debt, and assaults against newcomers. But at least the mainland didn't keep people in the endless limbo of the camp.

In spite of this, what was happening on Lesbos that summer wasn't considered a crisis by the UN. Without the crisis designation, people—citizens, funders, journalists—tended to look away. That was in part why I had come. I was often less interested in chasing a story at its boiling point than in what happened years later, when the attention had waned, when most of the cameras had turned away.

A bus lumbered into camp. The new arrivals, fresh from the dizzying sea, disembarked. A message was scrawled into the dust on the back window of the bus: *FUCK YOU.*

"If you asked me three weeks ago," Patric said, "I would say this is not a crisis. But now it is." All these arrivals and no transfers. "When there are no durable solutions for people, it is a crisis." A little boy walked by us wearing huge shoes, big enough for a man.

Patric had been with the UN since 2005. "Here's how I describe my job," he told us, though we hadn't asked. "I'm a vacuum cleaner after the war machine. It's a tragedy: death, destruction, devastation. I'm just a vacuum cleaner."

"One more," a woman in a Ministry of the Interior vest shouted to Patric, holding up a finger. As in: another boat had landed, and one more bus was on its way.

We thanked Patric and left the camp.

"They didn't show you the bad parts," Morteza said as we loaded back into the car. He meant "the jungle," where he himself lived—that true hell on earth where survival required the utmost vigilance and through which the fires would tear in just over a year's time.

We ate lunch at a small, near-empty restaurant in a small, near-empty town: fries and grilled sardines scooped from the bay. Morteza had been born in Afghanistan, but when he was a small child, his family fled to Iran. He wasn't able to build a life there, since he had no papers, but neither did he have proof of his Afghan citizenship, a set of circumstances that had him caught in an endless loop of flight and nonbelonging. Morteza's inner forearm was tattooed with a compass rose, resembling those that used to appear in the blank spaces of imperial maps.

"Some people have no country," he said. It was as simple as that, and it made all the difference in the world.

"The problem is the waiting," he explained. Every day was the same; it repeated and repeated. "It's like we're trapped in time." Morteza wanted to go to university—anywhere, he said, he didn't care where. He wanted to exit this purgatory of Moria, of Greece, for his life to re-begin, for a direction to reveal itself; he wanted to be on his way.

In the early days of the Lesbos arrivals, the refugee boats most often struck shore on the island's northern rim. Many towns there had been settled by Greeks from so-called Asia Minor, like the father of Vaselis the baker, who had come to Lesbos in 1922 from Anatolia—what is now Türkiye. As in Cyprus, where Pavlos was from, Greek-speaking Orthodox had lived for generations in Asia Minor among their Turkish-speaking Muslim neighbors; meanwhile, hundreds of thousands of Muslim Turkish speakers had been living in what was now known as Greece—borders being, after all, a fairly recent concept in the scale of human experience and in a sense figments of the imagination. The Greek and Turkish governments, long at odds, came to full-on war. The Greek army retreated from the city of Smyrna, where many Greek-speaking Orthodox had lived, and the Turkish forces gave the remaining Greek citizens an ultimatum: Leave or be killed. But how would they get out, all of a sudden, and all at once? The city was set on fire, and the Turks would soon rename it İzmir. As it burned, the fire devouring the Byzantine churches and storefronts and homes, people flooded to the shoreline. They were ignored by the American and British troops stationed in the harbor, though some were able to get out on fishing or military boats. Roughly 200,000 Greeks and Armenians fled Anatolia, and unknown thousands of others—50,000? 100,000?—stayed and were killed. In 1923, European authorities convened, along with the Turks and the Greeks, in Lausanne, to write a treaty that ended the war. The Greeks would go to Greece, the Turks to Türkiye, end of story.

It was in this way that boatloads of Greeks from Asia Minor had arrived on Lesbos's north shore, in what came to be known as "the Catastrophe," almost a hundred years before boatloads of Syrians and Afghans and Eritreans and others would begin to do the same.

It is often said that, as a result of the Catastrophe, Lesbos has a long history of welcoming foreigners to its shores. "But that's bullshit," Chloe Haralambous, a Greek advocate who helped found a welcome center for refugees on Lesbos, told me. "This island has a history of refugeehood, not a history of welcome." She showed me iconic photographs of the Asia Minor Greeks arriving at the northern shore of Lesbos, holding their babies, headscarves tied around their heads and bundles on their backs. "These are the mirror images of the contemporary refugee women holding babies, with bundles on their backs," she said.

Chloe invited me to her mother's house in the northern town of Klio to meet some of the town's elders, whose parents and grandparents had fled to Lesbos during the Catastrophe. We sat in Sappho's lush hillside garden, which looked out over the northern Aegean to the umber hills of Türkiye's coast. The elders arrived all at once, bearing sweets. There was Panos, a gregarious goat farmer in his eighties with bright eyes and hands so broad and steady that, in spite of his stoop, you felt as though they could build you a house; and Lilika and Annula, best friends in their seventies whose husbands had both died the year before. The widows still wore their mourning black: thick woolen skirts in spite of the heat, and stockings with sandals, just like my great-grandmother had worn.

Though the elders had never set foot in Asia Minor, they had been raised on stories of that homeland and all that had been lost when they'd had to leave: the acres of olive orchards, the ornate tapestries, the bundles of money hidden around the abandoned estates. When Annula's family fled, they hid coins in the seams of a cloth and used it to swaddle a newborn baby. One of the men carried the infant in his arms and swam out to meet the boat, so her cries wouldn't alert anyone to the boat leaving from shore. The baby lived, but the money proved useless; they couldn't exchange it for local currency once they got to Greece. The coins were just keepsakes now.

When they were small children, the elders all told me, their parents and grandparents sang them lullabies about their long-lost homes as they slid into sleep. Lilika had been raised in Klio, this very town where we sat, but true home seemed to be the mythic place of stories and songs across the sea. Each day she could look toward it: so close, so far away.

The elders told me that though some islanders had been up in arms when the refugees began coming in 2015, most of the Asia Minor Greeks in the north felt a kinship with the newest arrivals. "They asked me to protest," said Panos of some of his neighbors. "But I couldn't. I wouldn't. My grandmother had suffered the same things as these people."

Lilika nodded. "They were throwing rocks at our grandparents just as they are throwing rocks at the refugee boats today," she said.

At times, their reveries veered, as such stories tend to do, toward the realm of fabulism. Panos told us he had a cousin who had experienced a miracle on the other side of the island—a dream had instructed him where to take his sheep to keep them well. He'd also met a man who knew where to find an oracle nearby, one that showed a mirror into the future. The sheep themselves could see the future—once they'd run in advance of an earthquake, scattering to higher ground. In spite of his age, Panos still tended a herd of sheep on the hillside. He let them out of the barn to graze each morning and corralled them back in each night. He'd do it, he said, as his father had done: until the day he died.

That brought us back to Panos's family. As his father grew old, he began to slip back and forth in time. In Asia Minor, the family had narrowly escaped the Ottoman massacre and his father's sister, Anastasia, had been left behind. He never knew what became of her. In his final days, after coming down from the pasture, Panos's father would sing the sad songs from back home and speak to Anastasia as if she were alive. One day, on his sickbed, he opened his eyes. "Oh, Anastasia," the old man said to the empty space before him, "there you are. I've been wondering for so long where you'd gone."

When Panos's story was finished, Annula set down her spoon. "We know our family is gone," she said, "but every now and then my cousins and I get to talking and think, *What if someone from there showed up one day?*" She stared out into the distance toward Anatolia, as if imagining it.

Dusk was setting in, and it was time for everyone to head home. As we walked toward the front gate, Annula turned to me. "*Koukla,*" she said lovingly, taking my face in her hands. It was one of the few Greek words I'd learned as a kid—a term of endearment, directly translating to "doll," but meaning something like "beautiful sweetheart." Evanthia had taught it to me. I couldn't help it; my eyes welled up with tears. No one had taken my face in their hands and called me *koukla* since my grandmother had died.

"Come to my home next time," said Annula. "I, too, have a garden, and a yard. I'll make you coffee and tell you more stories."

A few days later, Thi and I drove back south, the mountainous hills giving way to a broad wetland valley and a salty marsh populated with hundreds upon hundreds of flamingos: migrants stopping over on their way south to Africa. If you'd told me I would encounter such bright pink absurdities on this dry island in Greece, I would have thought you were spinning a tall tale, the kind the Greek side of my family always liked to tell. But here they were, carpeting the bog like an overnight bloom.

15.

Every time I was in Greece, it seemed, some fresh new horror from back home swept the headlines: people dying in the desert and drowning in the Rio Grande, children in cages, a record number of kids stuck in immigration detention. This time, as Thi and I conducted our interviews all over Lesbos, news broke that the Trump administration was continuing to take children from their parents at the US–Mexico border and cramming them into filthy, freezing, overcrowded cells.

There was another, less-covered story that caught my attention: Scott Warren, of the organization No More Deaths, was facing federal charges for his humanitarian work in the Arizona borderlands. For years, Warren and other No More Deaths volunteers had trekked through the desert to leave water and provisions so that migrants passing through might survive the journey. Out there, it wasn't uncommon to happen across the dead; when he did, Warren often performed a quiet, solemn ritual over their bodies. In 2018, he was arrested on charges of conspiracy and harboring unauthorized immigrants. He and several other volunteers were also charged with the federal crime of littering—the trash, in this case, being the bottles full of lifesaving water.

Since the nineties, the United States has embraced an immigration policy of prevention through deterrence: the more deadly the crossing, the more hostile the treatment upon being detained, the thinking goes, the fewer people will try to come, having heard what horrors await them. Greece, like the rest of Europe in general, was employing similar strategies in an attempt to scare people sedentary.

But these tactics never work. The infamous US border wall—really just a collection of unconnected barricades—was built in areas that were easier to cross. It didn't dissuade people from coming, only pushed them into harsher and more deadly territory. In the early 2000s, the US government continued to criminalize and "crack down" on human smuggling, which only succeeded in making the journey more expensive, upped the stakes of the crossing, and helped to fuse the moving of people with the moving of drugs. None of the obstacles—walls, surveillance, prolonged and inhumane detention, family separation, laws criminalizing migration and human smuggling—deterred people from crossing to the United States, and deterrence wasn't working in Europe, either. The tactics simply increased the likelihood that, whether in the Mediterranean or in the Sonoran Desert, a person would die trying.

Now, in the case of Scott Warren, the US government was expanding its criminalizing reach. From my bed by the window in Greece, I read that the jury in Warren's case was hung eight to four in favor of his innocence and that there would be a retrial.

By the end of the year, 497 deaths would be confirmed along the US–Mexico border—a number that of course included only the bodies that had been found. The same year, at least 1,885 people would die in the Mediterranean. European governments and EU authorities were, just like in the United States, now also criminalizing those who attempted to provide humanitarian assistance.

While crossing from Türkiye to Lesbos is a journey of many terrifying hours, crossing from North Africa into Italy or Spain can take days and is far more deadly. An organization called Sea-Watch performs search-and-rescue operations by ship and plane, monitoring the waters that the EU and its member countries often neglect or refuse to patrol. Claiming that the organization is a human-smuggling operation rather than a rescue mission, some European governments have secretly investigated its volunteers, tried to shut down their operations, and barred its ships from docking with rescued crossers who, had it not been for Sea-Watch, would have drowned.

"You're not allowed to enter port," Pia Klemp, a German biologist who volunteers as a captain with Sea-Watch, told *The Intercept*. "You're not allowed to leave port, ships are confiscated, flags withdrawn, crew investigated." While Scott Warren was awaiting retrial, Klemp was facing criminal charges in Italy. These cases felt to me like the newest act in the elaborate theater of the contemporary border zone.

Thi and I visited a restaurant on the island called Home for All. It was run by Ekaterina Koveou and Nikos Katsouris, a Greek couple who had transformed their small taverna into a place to cook for refugees living in the camps. Each day Katerina and Nikos served dozens of newly arrived refugees a fresh-cooked meal in the restaurant and packed their trucks full of food for people living in Moria. They, too, had been targeted by authorities for operating without a proper nonprofit permit, and they had been intimidated by local anti-immigration thugs. Even some friends and neighbors had complained: Why were they helping refugees, which only encouraged more people to come? What about helping their fellow Greeks?

"It doesn't matter," Katerina told me of their gripes. Her work was a matter of basic morals, she felt, nonnegotiable.

The restaurant is situated on a quiet harbor in the Bay of Gera. The first evening Thi and I visited, we sat outside listening to Katerina and

Nikos's stories of dealing with a hostile government and the ill-equipped UN and NGOs. I noticed a few dozen jars of purple-red liquid sitting on outdoor tables beneath the waning sun—herbal infusions of some kind, I guessed upon a closer look. I asked Katerina what they were.

She couldn't remember the name in English, so she said it in Greek instead, and described the plant—a yellow, scrubby flower that thrived in the dry, open hills.

"This one?" I asked, showing her a picture of the flowers I'd been so entranced by on Andros.

"Yes," she told me, "that's the one." With the Greek name, we looked up the flower in English: hypericum, or Saint-John's-wort. It also grew wild here on Lesbos, and each summer Katerina foraged and made infusions with the plant for its therapeutic properties. When it was packed in oil, the liquid turned the color of blood. Of late she'd been making larger batches to offer to the refugees. "It's good for the mood," she said. "Helps with depression and sorrow."

I asked Katerina whether this flower gave off the sweet fragrance I'd noticed on the hillsides. It did, she confirmed. The weirdest thing, I confessed to her as if it were a secret, was that every time I had bent my head to the yellow flowers on Andros, the scent vanished.

"Yes," she confirmed again. "You cannot smell it when you want to. It's all around, but it hides when you go near." And although hypericum grew wild all over these loamy hills, it was difficult to cultivate. That's what she liked about it, she told me. "This is a plant that is strong and does exactly what she wants."

Thi left Lesbos for a few days to pick up her son. I spent the time alone in the northern part of the island, thinking and writing and sitting by the water where the black urchins flashed beneath the surface, as they had on the banks of Hydra. I was accumulating words in Greek now: *good morning, good afternoon, mermaid, sea, boat.* Early each morning in the small town where I slept, a team of international volunteers loaded up on a pontoon to trawl the sea for shipwrecks. I read more about hypericum, the yellow flower, how ancients considered it a bearer of light, how it was gathered and burned at the summer solstice to ward off bad spirits. I took walks in the hills and kept my eyes out for it, but it seemed to appear only when I wasn't searching. One afternoon I roamed lazily into an artisan shop, where I found an evil eye fused from pale blue and green glass, frayed nautical rope dangling from it like jellyfish tentacles. I bought it and, in superstition, laid it near my bed.

There'd been another shipwreck; seven people from the Republic of Congo drowned within swimming distance to shore before a rescue boat arrived. None of the passengers knew how to swim, and their life jackets had been fakes.

"I can't stop thinking about them," one survivor told me of her companions who had perished. She was haunted by the way they gulped their final breaths before disappearing beneath the water.

So much reporting of humanitarian catastrophe involves statistics and scale, but the magnitude of such numbers quickly dissolves into abstraction. Over a million people had crossed to Lesbos in the past four years, sometimes several thousand in a single day. As a journalist, I know that these numbers both make meaning and obscure it. There's something useful about this dynamic to the larger politic—the numbers serve as an escape hatch dressed up as facts, the spare clarity of data veiling the specificity of suffering that might otherwise be too much to bear. Even so, it is the job of a journalist to offer particulars within the abstraction, to help a reader conceive of this inconceivable scale.

One method: visit the old dump on the north side of Lesbos, where two mounds of decaying life vests once towered several times a person's height, drooping a bit more each day as the elements softened the heap like an enormous corpse. Life Vest Mountain, as this place had come to be known, was never on any official map but marked the landscape like a topographical feature; before it was bulldozed in 2021, the locals all knew of its existence and where to find it, not far from the popular tourist town of Molyvos.

Thi took me up to Life Vest Mountain one day when the wind wailed and packs of goats grazed amid the thistles and scrub. Some of the life vests were torn to expose counterfeit flotation material, some were still buckled tight, as if upon a body now invisible. There were towering masses of other items, too: the occasional single shoe, an infant car seat, tangled fishing nets, a knit hat, deflated pontoons, a winter coat for an adult and another for a small child, a shredded Mylar party balloon, empty water bottles, a board pierced with rusted nails and spattered with red and blue paint, like an insurrectionist flag. I spotted a vacuum cleaner, presumably no longer functioning. *A vacuum cleaner after the war machine.*

On the outskirts of the mounds were a dozen or so discarded boats. They looked in good enough shape to float, even to make it across the stretch of water to Türkiye, and I wondered what unseen wound had relegated them here. There were engine covers scattered among the ruins, brands I'd never heard of—Yamabisi, Power Tec. All their casings were cracked. As I circumnavigated the mounds, I came to a place where ten of these engine husks had been arranged in a perfect circle like an installation or a memorial.

Life Vest Mountain was both a clarification of scale and a further abstraction. Out of context, the items were just fodder for the imagination. And the place had become a tourist attraction, a stop along the disaster trail. I found myself trying to connect the dots, piecing together presumptive narratives of doom as well as salvation from the discarded things.

"All archaeology really means is we're studying the past through material traces," explains the anthropologist Jason De León. He runs the Undocumented Migration Project in the southwestern United States, where his team studies recent traces of migration through the desert. This project, he explains, demonstrates "that archaeology as a tool to understand the human condition does not have to be sequestered in the distant past." What of the ruins of yesterday, or this morning? After more than a decade recording what has been left in the desert, his team has noted differences in the kinds of belongings that migrants now carry and leave behind. Where once they found items that spoke of some imagined future—fancy dresses, toys, hair curlers—they now find predominantly relics of bare survival: backpacks, broken shoes, socks, emptied water bottles.

Like other social sciences, archaeology thinks of itself as capable of securing definitive answers—even though we know, as De León points out, that "artifacts lie all the time," as with the sculptures left from ancient Greece. He observes that history has a tendency to whitewash, and that the remains of the borderlands risk suffering the fate of Ellis Island: becoming a touristic monument to history, with the grave injustices and human rights abuses that occurred there muffled. Any artifact risks becoming a simple, static story.

De León's team often finds relics of prayer at the border: votives positioned in desert washes, prayer cards slid into the pants pockets of people who are captured or who die. An entire pantheon watches over migrants: Saint John Baptist Scalabrini, who dedicated the latter part of his life to supporting European immigrants; Saint Frances Cabrini, named the patron of migrants by the pope in 1950; Saint Toribio Romo González, a Catholic martyr, who is said to appear in the desert as a blue-eyed helper, offering water and guiding the way. In many places, the US border apparatus traverses ancient burial grounds and violates sites sacred to Indigenous peoples. In this way, observes the writer Marcello de Cintio, "the walls wound ancient ritual as well as breed new saints."

"I had to put my faith in God," a teenager from Gambia once told me of his long crossing from Libya to Sicily, in a boat so overpacked that, if a person so much as shifted his weight, the whole rig could go down. A rescue ship arrived just in time; the edges of the vessel had already begun to swamp. "Only God could save me," this young man said of the crossing. And in his mind, through the work of these rescuers, God did.

I issued a prayer for the dead up on Life Vest Mountain, which I imagined was carried away on the wind. Then Thi and I got back in the car and drove to a rocky beach where we floated for a while and rid ourselves of the smell of trash. But even as I fell asleep that night, swaying with the memory of my body on the waves, I caught whiffs of the refuse, and the image of that eerie circle of cracked engines stayed with me, the dizzying dimensions of what remained.

16.

That summer of 2019, Greece proposed a border intervention resembling something from an absurdist novel: to stop the refugees from coming, the government would build a floating wall that stretched across the surface of the sea.

Greece was not the only country building preposterous walls as an assertion of power and a display of sovereignty. In recent years, more border walls have been built and proposed than ever in the history of the nation-state; there were seven at the end of World War II, and by the time Trump was on the campaign trail there were more than seventy. This tells us something about the tremulousness of the contemporary nation-state. "What we have come to call the globalized world," writes Wendy Brown, "harbors fundamental tensions between opening and barricading, fusion and partition, erasure and reinscription." A border, like whiteness, like the state, is a fiction of grave consequences. It's an imaginary absolute that bisects a landscape, turning terrain into territory. The border: the most tyrannical line of all.

I've always been drawn to borders: their paradox, their physicality, their kinetic dynamism. US passport stored safely in my pocket, I am able to sit at a border all day long and have done so, as if by staring for long enough I might decode the twin human impulses: to divide and to cross over.

Once, I went to learn about a tiny, much-contested border wall in the Arctic. Northernmost Norway was a strange place to consider borders, for it is a landscape where land meets sea, water meets ice, taiga forest meets open tundra. Even the membrane between day and night shifts dramatically from day to day: there are days without darkness and other days when the sun barely glimmers at the horizon.

Here, in the summer of 2015, refugees, mostly from Syria and Afghanistan, began crossing from Russia into Norway just a few miles from the town of Kirkenes. They took this route to a safe, prosperous country in order to avoid the deadly bottleneck of Greece and other countries in southern Europe. The travelers found their way to the Russian city of Murmansk, where they hid out in local hotels and hired smugglers to help them reach the other side. A treaty between Russia and Norway prohibits crossing the border on foot, so the smugglers furnished bicycles, which were far cheaper than cars. Word got out and more people made the journey, racing the coming winter. By November, when the Arctic was cloaked in snow, more than 5,500 migrants from some fifty countries had crossed over on bicycle into a town of 10,000 people. Because the cheap bicycles weren't up to Norwegian safety codes, they had to be discarded once they'd rolled across the border. A pile of bikes as high as a building towered on the Norwegian side, reminiscent of Life Vest Mountain.

As on Lesbos, the Kirkenes community mostly supported the new arrivals, opening up spaces in their homes and community centers for them to sleep, ensuring they were fed and cared for. But outside the border region, it was a different story. A nationalist movement was flourishing in a country known for its progressive policies—a movement that sowed fears of a disappearing Nordic race. While Norway took in refugees every year, it was always on the government's terms and timeline. Now, in the eyes of some Norwegians, the border was being breached.

Forced migrants often become a political hot potato, and this was no exception. The Norwegian government claimed that the refugees were Russia's problem, and set out to deport hundreds of them back to the other side. One winter night, Norwegian authorities deposited a Syrian mother and her two small children to the east of Norway's border. It was dark and snowing. The woman sat down with her kids in the middle of the no-man's-land between the two checkpoints and refused to move. After some time, the authorities succeeded in forcing her on.

Eventually, after several months of debate, Russian border agents stopped letting people out. The word got out on social media, and the refugees stopped coming. "They disappeared," said the mayor of Nikel, the Russian town on the other side of the border from Kirkenes. Then, four months after the last asylum seeker had crossed into this region of Norway, the Ministry of Justice in Oslo made the determination that Norway needed a wall there.

Throughout time, humans have erected walls to bolster a sense of security and grandeur and might; the infamous Great Wall of China was actually some 2,500 miles of semiconnected segments and additional barriers built to keep out the Mongolians. In the second century CE, the Roman emperor Hadrian conceived of a seventy-mile stone fortification at the upper reach of his empire—now in the United Kingdom—in order to manage trade, keep out the barbarians, and project the power of his empire and his own might as a ruler. The Incan empire was fortified with gilded walls.

While impressive as architectural monuments and symbols of repression, these border walls all largely failed in their express purpose. Guards along the Great Wall of China were often bribed to gain entry; "barbarians" breached Hadrian's wall and killed a general and his troops. Walls have never really worked—there's almost always some way over, under, or through—yet we build them all the same.

What drew me to the wall in Norway was that it was so tiny and so remote, yet the subject of so much ardor and vitriol. Border walls, writes Brown, are "screens for a host of projected desires, needs, or anxieties." A wall is most powerful in its symbolism—and indeed, myths and legends are full of them. A wall separates the Babylonian lovers Pyramus and Thisbe in Ovid's *Metamorphoses*; the walls of the city of Troy are so sturdy that the only way in is via trickery and a massive wooden horse. Norse mythology tells of the time that the gods accidentally hired a giant, masquerading as a pilgrim, to build a protective wall around their kingdom in exchange for a goddess's hand in marriage, as well as possession of the sun and the moon. The territories on the other side of these walls are so valuable, the thinking goes, that people want in at any cost—and the worst of the invaders will come disguised as something benign.

Like the walls in these old myths, today's walls function, above all, as a form of storytelling. "It's important to send signals," Espen Teigen, then an adviser in the Norwegian Ministry of Immigration and Integration, told me. No matter that the refugees had stopped coming by the time the wall was built, he said. The wall was a signal that Norway was closed.

Yet walls can have a corrosive effect on the society they purportedly protect. Inside the walls, society becomes closed and highly policed, as do the identities of those within. "When do the new walls become more like the confining walls of a prison, rather than the comforting walls of a house?" Brown asks. "When does the fortress become a penitentiary?"

I visited Norway's Storskog border checkpoint on a cold, clear day in late winter when everything in view sparkled with sunlight and ice.

Like many contemporary border fortifications, the Norwegian barrier is actually more of a fence. Construction on the Storskog fence was completed in 2016. It now stands right across from an old Soviet barricade once meant to keep people in. For this is another function of walls, from East Germany to North Korea to Palestine to the Mur de la Peste, or Plague Wall, in Marseille, or the wall the Greek government threatened to build around Moria: to prevent people from leaving. The old Arctic barricade had been recently updated with Russian surveillance cameras. On the frozen cusp of northern Europe, the two fences stood opposite each other, as if in face-off.

Outside the checkpoint, the ground was an uneven crackle of crystalline ice that splintered underfoot. And there, across a frozen lake, was Russia, dappled with petite birch trees and Arctic spruce. It looked just like Norway except with the sheen of magic that came with being a designated elsewhere. For me, borders have an uncanny atmosphere of temptation; that day, for instance, I worried I might accidentally find myself in Russia, in violation of international law, as if the border were a vortex with subliminal pull. Milan Kundera once described vertigo much the same way: not so much the fear of falling, but the dizziness caused by a secret desire to jump. Who doesn't want to put their toes across the line, just to feel it?

Inside the station, I met with border chief Stein Kristian Hansen. He thought that the international attention the wall had drawn—including, presumably, my visit—was something of a tempest in a teapot. What was all the fuss? Hansen was a rare local in favor of the fence, but mostly because the design included a retractable gate—one he could, in case of emergency, open and close with the touch of a button. He was certain that the fence would do nothing to curb any future flow of refugees. "And it will do nothing to stop Putin."

He took me out to see it, this partition I'd traveled all this way to behold. It was only slightly more formidable than a schoolyard fence, made of tight chain link secured to metal posts that sliced a path through the low boreal forest. The trees had been razed about ten feet on either side, allowing for a clear view in case, say, anyone tried to make a run for it. To our right, Lake Näsijärvi formed a natural boundary. On our left, the fence crested a slight hill and disappeared from sight, creating the impression that it continued on forever, though Hansen explained that it stopped just a few yards past where we could see.

The slatted metal gate that Hansen had advocated for was open, a gaping mouth between where the no-man's-land ended and Norway began. With mechanized wheels, it was designed to slide shut across the tarmac. Unfortunately, Hansen explained, the design was off: the bottom edge wasn't high enough to clear the snowpack, so, at the onset of winter, the gate had quickly frozen into place. For now, they kept it open at all times.

"They'll rebuild it during the summer," he said with a shrug, giving the fence a final little jiggle. We turned our backs on Russia and, our breath freezing against our faces, went inside to get warm.

My mom had always wanted to visit Norway, so she decided to join me for part of the trip. As it happened, my brother's DNA test had also determined a 1.7 percent Norwegian heritage, meaning that someone, far back and likely on my mother's side, had come from Norway. This was deemed mere genetic curiosity rather than some token of belonging. Identity is sourced from community and connection and knowledge of a people's stories, not solely, as many Indigenous leaders in the United States insist, from blood quantum, or the simple fact of DNA. It didn't occur to us to imagine ourselves as wayward ancestors, returned.

Between my reporting commitments, we'd made plans to visit a hotel built of ice. In the wooden lodge of the Kirkenes snow hotel, a young woman ushered us from the well-heated lodge to the basement, where subzero-rated sleeping bags hung on wooden pegs and the hollow cold seeped through a set of double doors leading to the wing of the hotel that was built entirely from snow. "This way," she said, opening the doors and beckoning us through, the cold swallowing us whole.

We emerged into a narrow, arched grotto of ice, then into a dimly lit corridor, eerie and grand, that echoed like the halls of an old stone abbey. "Welcome to the snow hotel!" chirped our guide. The hallway led to a dozen separate guest rooms, each with a large bed sculpted from ice and walls carved with ornate, fantastical imagery, as if the setting for a fairy tale. One room was nautical-themed, the great wheel of a ship hovering above the bedside and a mermaid peeking from the corner; another room was encased in an uncanny thicket of twisting trees. A garish purple-pink light illuminated each room, but other than that the snow hotel, so over-the-top and strange in its craftsmanship and purpose, was truly beautiful. And that night, save for us, it was empty.

To stay there required gearing up in heavy clothing and burrowing into those colossal sleeping bags. It wasn't as cold as it looked, though, our guide assured us. To sleep within this ice was something of a paradox: out on the tundra, the temperatures could kill you, but inside, the ice, as Indigenous people have known for millennia, could provide warmth, protection, a place to lay your head—home.

"No, thank you," said my mother.

The hallway opened to a gaping central chamber that resembled a cocktail lounge, with a grand bar and stools fashioned from ice. We sat there for a while, imagining this space full of people warming themselves with liquor and cast in the strange glow of the light, the ice, the steam of their breath blurring their features. It was like picturing a party for ghosts.

We asked the woman from the hotel what happened to the place once the temperatures warmed. Oh, she replied, in springtime they just let it melt. It was now the middle of March. Soon, this lavish, baffling structure would begin to soften and buckle, becoming, eventually, a mound of slush—all the carvings liquefied, the adornments gone. The hotel staff would clear the heap and scatter it over the fields, where it would melt into something ungraspable, absorbed into the thawing land. And then next year they'd start all over again.

What we were standing in, then, was ephemera, most exquisite because it was temporary. It was a tourist gimmick, but also a creation in playful conversation with the landscape and the seasons and the passing of time.

Seated on the stools made of ice in the hotel's empty bar, I thought of the architect Ronald Rael's ecstatic *Borderwall as Architecture: A Manifesto for the U.S.-Mexico Boundary*. Crafted in response to the US government's request for proposals for the border wall, the book presents a series of speculative designs at once absurdist and moving: a cactus wall, for instance, to help restore eviscerated habitat, a wastewater-treatment wall, a solar wall to generate power. Other designs are more mischievous: a wally ball, where the border doubles as a net; a climbing wall; and a Teeter-Totter Wall ("People on both sides could directly experience the interdependency between the two countries"). There's the wall where you could confess your sins to a listener across the border, or the lunch counter where people on opposite sides of the line can share a meal. A library wall would allow people to pass books back and forth; a wall whose slats are tuned like those of a xylophone could transform division into music.

The book is a form of protest, for to imagine such exultant utility of a border wall is to interrupt a border's indifferent bifurcation. "The need to reimagine the border through the logic of natural and social systems is the foremost challenge for the future of this binational region and of many other border regions across the globe," writes the architect Teddy Cruz. These proposals are attempts to render metaphors and meaning from the wall that transcend and transform its function of division.

My mother and I left the snow hotel and walked across a frozen field to a small hut where we put on snowsuits that resembled space gear and were handed the keys to a snowmobile. We wanted to go out onto the darkened tundra in search of the northern lights. My mother piloted the vessel into the night with me tucked in behind her, our eyes lifted upward as we rumbled forward. Our growling engine disrupted the vast quiet, but when we turned it off it felt as if we were hovering in the crisp, blackened infinite where it was impossible to discern where the iced-over world ended and sky began. And soon they appeared: the northern lights performing their eerie, incandescent churn. The lights would tear through the night for a while and then vanish, only to appear again in some other part of the sky.

This astronomical phenomenon has signified many things to many people across time and space: tidings of good fortune, portent of war, the advent of a child. I was shivering, and my toes had gone numb, but I had no desire to turn back just yet. I was thrilled to be stationed beneath that infinite sky, disoriented in the ceaseless, undivided night.

Each day in Kirkenes was noticeably longer than the last, as if we were watching the earth tilting on its axis as we spun. My last night, I joined the staff of the local newspaper at their tidy office in the center of town for happy hour. We crowded into the small room, pulling up folding chairs and cracking open beers. As the sun lowered in the sky, Brede, the building's landlord, suggested a nightcap at his place and a chance to see what he called his "bunker." I was curious. So the six of us followed him through downtown, where dusk cast pale cornflower light onto the snow-heaped rooftops. Brede led us into his backyard and along a neatly shoveled pathway through hip-high snow. He knelt down to the ground and, with a grunt, yanked up a great metal door.

"Here," our host bellowed theatrically, with a slight backward sway, "is my bunker!"

A staircase descended more than a story underground and deposited us into a great, reverberating cavern that brought to mind an apocalyptic ballroom. Wide as a school auditorium and with ceilings towering more than twenty feet, the bunker's main chamber connected to half a dozen other rooms, some blocked by metal doors, others accessible via a low-ceilinged hallway.

Brede explained that the structure had been dug by the Nazis during World War II. It was just a small part of what was once a massive municipal underworld. "There are bunkers all over Kirkenes," one of the local journalists told me, "but I've never seen anything like this."

Brede tossed us each another beer and called us over to a narrow circular stone chamber that reached all the way up to the surface of the earth above us; looking up, we could catch a glimpse of the evening light. He had discovered this tubular room only the year before, when a crack running beneath one of the bunker's walls inspired him to take it down with a jackhammer. The room was filled with the garbage that he and his family had been dumping down a mystery hole in the backyard for decades. "We thought there might be treasure," Brede said, laughing, "but it was just my own trash!" He slammed his hand against another wall, beyond which further mystery lay. "This summer, I'm going to knock it down."

My bunker companions were unanimously against the Kirkenes border wall—it was an absurdist joke, for one. But also, geographically and socially, many in the town felt far more connected to their neighbors in Russia—just a few hours' drive away—than to the capital of Norway, which they could reach only by plane or by dozens of hours of driving, crossing in and out of Finland. The wall had nothing to do with the people of Kirkenes—it was a project of Oslo, of the interior. Border regions are often both the pawns of geopolitics and their battlegrounds.

There was a historical dimension to this town's connection with Russia, too. During World War II, the Nazis had controlled Norway, and Kirkenes, on the front line, was one of the most-bombed towns in all of Europe (hence all the bunkers). It was the Soviet Union that had liberated Norway from the Nazis—an act not soon forgotten. The promise of postwar Europe was one of opening, not of division. To my Norwegian companions, the new shutting of the border between Russia and Norway wasn't just farcical but also dangerous: an act of retrograde closure presaging who knew what kind of social order. In just a few years time, it would be Russia that flouted its own border with Ukraine, waging war in an attempt to rewrite the map and claim more territory as its own. Millions of people would be forced to flee their homes as a result.

Forced migrants are seeking refuge around the world in record numbers, and the refugee crises are steadily moving toward the global North, into wealthier countries like Norway and the United States and even debt-saddled Greece, places long defined by an insistence on well-defined borders. Meanwhile, the nation-state itself is in crisis. If a nation seems to be coming apart, perhaps a wall can hold it together. A populace can convince itself that it is in a condition of perpetual siege—can turn the state into a bunker.

17.

After that first trip to Greece in 2019, I returned to California and hung the nautical evil eye in my kitchen, where I caught sight of it each morning as I started the kettle for tea. Where I had scoured the news from home while in Greece, I now did the reverse, staying glued to what was happening on Lesbos and in the Mediterranean at large. None of the news was good.

Two weeks later, I traveled to Tijuana for another magazine assignment. Earlier that year, the Trump administration had effectively shuttered the border by creating a metering system that required asylum seekers to wait on the Mexican side for the chance to cross and apply for protection, only to be returned across the border, via a sinisterly named Trump-era policy, the Migrant Protection Protocols, to wait in Mexico for their next court date—which could be months or even years away. Only so many people would be allowed across each morning—the number changed daily, depending on the whims of the US Border Patrol. Once across, the migrants could request asylum in the United States, after which most of them would be returned to Mexico for another long, long wait as their cases progressed. Having traveled so far—from El Salvador, Guatemala, Haiti, the Republic of Congo, Cameroon, Pakistan—these asylum seekers showed up at the border and were assigned a number on an informal ledger. The ledger was managed by a volunteer, also an asylum seeker waiting for their number to be called, and when it came to their own turn to cross, they would pass the job off to another volunteer down the line. When I visited in July, dozens of people queued up each morning, often with suitcases in hand, hoping their time had come. By then, the wait was roughly four months long.

My friend Hannah, a nurse, came with me to Tijuana, both of us bringing bags packed full of donated medical supplies. There are few steadfast, enforceable rules of journalism, but most magazines prohibit—or strongly discourage—journalists from offering assistance to the people they are writing about, out of a sense that doing so flouts objectivity, and that it will change the course of the story observed. Under the circumstances, this stricture seemed absurd. We carried the bags through the border checkpoint at San Ysidro, where helicopters circled overhead and the turnstiles issued a menacing *clunk* each time a person passed through to the other side.

Hannah spent the next few days giving medical exams to people huddled in the dozens of shelters that peppered the city while I went around asking questions. *How long have you been here? How long did it take you to get here? What is it like to live here, what is your plan, how long do you expect to wait, what do you hope for when you cross to the other side?* There were journalists all over Tijuana now, and many of the people I met had already been interviewed at some point along their journey north, if not many times. For many of them, it was plain, the telling had become wearisome. Again, I felt extractive. I envied Hannah, who had something real to offer: medical skills, supplies, and advice—things people actually needed.

As I'd reflected at Life Vest Mountain, such catastrophes tend to reduce people to mere numbers: in the news, in the lines at the border, in local politics, even on the clipboards in the medical tents. *What does it feel like to be treated like a number?* is perhaps what I should have been asking.

We stayed only a few days. School started again in August; a third of my school's students were in active deportation proceedings, and many of them still needed lawyers. *Do you need a lawyer?* we would ask new students. *When is your next court date?* My colleagues and I would do the math, counting down the days. We looked at their paperwork. *How old are you?* Once they turned eighteen, it would be difficult for them to qualify for certain kinds of immigration relief, meaning they were racing a ticking clock. Numbers upon numbers. Stuck in line in Tijuana, people wanted the numbers to move quickly so they could make it to the front of the line. But on the other side, it was the opposite: people wished that time would slow. *What is your alien number?* We showed students and their families how to dial an automated 1-800 hotline and input their nine-digit alien registration number in order to hear an automated voice announce the date and time of their next court date—subject to change at any time.

Months passed like this, with the Trump administration instituting policy after policy to eviscerate asylum protections and put asylum seekers further at risk. In March 2020, over our school's spring break, I had tickets to go back to Greece. My plan was to travel overland through the Balkans and into Greece, passing across the contested borders that I'd spent so much time staring at on maps. But as the pandemic reared up, my trip was, naturally, canceled. The district announced that school was closing for two weeks. On March 13, the day before lockdown was to begin, I went around to all the classrooms with a clipboard in hand, kneeling next to each student to ask for their cell phone numbers so we'd be able to stay in contact until the school opened again. (It would be more than a year.)

Now there were new numbers to obsess over: there were 342 COVID deaths reported on that last day of school; just a month later, 5,700 would die in a single day. The Trump administration shut the border, fully this time. The metering line stopped. But it struck me that the virus was the opposite of a border wall. Here the virus was all around us, in a way, connecting us all.

The week after school shut down in Oakland and throughout the country and throughout the world, I fell sick, a sickness I confused at first with the grief of the moment. But then came the chills and the fever, and my throat swelled as if it were crammed with stones. I slept when I could, sometimes deeply, sometimes not at all, inert in my bed, unable to do much as the virus unfurled through me like a lace. The city shut down, and many of our students and their families lost their jobs—most of them in the restaurant industry or driving for Lyft and Uber.

These months were even more ruled by numbers. I spent weeks sick in bed, steeped again in numbers that I input into forms as I helped families apply for unemployment: dates of birth, hourly wages, hours worked per week, Social Security numbers. I called the California unemployment hotline so often that I memorized the number, even though the line was almost always busy or unanswered.

"I only have thirteen dollars in my bank account," one father told me over the phone as we filled out his application. He had been a tailor in Senegal but had worked as a rideshare driver for the past few years. Now stuck at home, he'd made dozens of cloth masks, which, at the time, were in short supply. "I'm just at home, what else do I have to do?" he said. He wanted to donate them to the school, so that the staff distributing food during lockdown would have protection. All of his masks, I noticed when I picked them up, were made with material emblazoned with the US flag.

From my bed, when I wasn't raising money for direct assistance and filing unemployment applications, I read about the pandemic and then, to distract myself from that, I read about the rise of the neo-Nazi party in Greece—its own deadly virus. My phone pinged with calendar reminders of where I was supposed to be: "Hungary." "Serbia." "Macedonia." "Greece." On the day I was meant to arrive on Lesbos, I read that a group of fascists had attacked the main refugee camp on the island, taking bludgeons to the cars of aid workers, setting the refugees' dwellings on fire. It made me think of the Omaha mobs forcing the Greek residents to flee, how history circles back on itself like a snake.

I called my parents on FaceTime. The night before, in a burst of energy that took hold when my fever subsided, I had traveled through an internet wormhole related to our ancestry. I finally figured out where Evanthia had been born: a town called Korthio on Andros island. Ben and I hadn't ventured that far south, not even close. It struck me as sad, and then hilarious, to have traveled all that way and missed it.

I told all this to my father, but, unfamiliar as he was with the specifics of the landscape, it didn't mean much to him. For him, Greece was Greece, where we were from. So he countered with a tale of his own. "Have I ever told you the story about the land?"

We are a family of raconteurs, but my father is the emperor of fabulists and the best storyteller of all. By now, I'd heard dozens, if not hundreds, of his stories. That a new tale could appear out of the ether was a marvel.

"The land?" I asked.

He told me that his aunt Tula, my grandmother's beloved sister who died young, had once come upon a dusty old trunk in Evanthia's attic. She opened it (who wouldn't?) and found it full of papers. There was one particularly tattered document that stood out to her, official-looking and written in Greek. Though Tula spoke Greek well enough, she couldn't read it, so she asked her mother what it said.

"Oh, that?" my great-grandmother said. She hunched over to read it. "That is a will."

My dad was a bad kid growing up—stealing cars, jumping out the window in the middle of class to skip school, filching cigarettes, and once even turning the school bell upside down and filling it with water so that, by the next morning, it had frozen solid and no one made it to class on time. His father, who had grown up poor, often chastised him for his wayward behavior. "You'll end up shining shoes in Trenton!" he'd bellow. His mother, raised with the respectability pressures of new immigrants, didn't know what to do with him, either. But Tula adored my dad and believed in him, so anytime she shows up in my father's stories it's a signal that we may be veering from history into improvisation—into a story that may be true in feeling but perhaps less than so in its every fact. That is to say, into myth.

"A will!" Tula exclaimed to her mother. "What does it say?"

My great-grandmother read the tattered paper: it said that she had inherited two acres of land on an island in the Cyclades.

"This is great!" Tula exclaimed. Where there was land there was money—or at the very least, the possibility of such.

"Wait, wait," my great-grandmother said. There was a catch. In order to redeem this inheritance, Evanthia had to present herself at some office or other in Greece, in person, within twenty years of the letter's issuance. She and Tula did the math: exactly twenty-one years had passed. The numbers didn't lie. It was too late; the land was long gone.

"Wow," I said, when my father was finished with his story.

"Two acres on Greece's primo island!" he said. "We'd be rich!"

I countered that Andros wasn't exactly one of Greece's "primo" islands but that it was, indeed, beautiful.

"No, no, it wasn't Andros—it was Mykonos!" he said. The partygoers' paradise where, in an attempt to spin the land into gold, as I had seen with my own eyes, it had all been wrung dry.

But our family had been peasants—farmers and sailmakers—and from a completely different island (though, to be fair, not far from Mykonos). This whole story smacked of fairy tale: the buried treasure, the dusty trunk, the hidden message, the allure of transformation, the thwarted dreams. "It's a great story, Dad, but it can't really be true."

"It is true!" he insisted. He hated when my brother and I fact-checked his stories, that he had such spoilsports for kids. "It is absolutely true!

"All I know," he said, "is that that is what the lore of our family was, and so that is what the letter said." In other words: when a story has been passed through the generations and told again and again, the repetition—and the story's survival—is the very thing that makes it true. And sick as I was, and filled with longing to be somewhere other than my bed—to be in a different world—it was nice to have a good story to pass the time. *What else am I going to do?*

My great-grandmother had once been an entry on a ship's manifest, a person in line, an alien waiting to be processed, someone without citizenship but with a number that determined, in the eyes of officials, who she was. The longer an immigrant family lives here, the less of a number its members become. I get to be a full person in the United States of America, this place like a dusty trunk stuffed with old and new hopes, true and untrue stories—a white person who belongs, now, barely a number at all.

PART III

Future

18.

In those early months of COVID, people continued to hover in the unknown, wondering what was safe and what might be deadly, and yearning to know what the future held for this apocalyptic world. News—journalism—became a lifeline, but also fuel for more anxiety and fear. I stayed glued to my phone, not only in search of reliable information about the virus but in order to follow what was happening in Greece: refugees penned inside Moria, clashes between the NGOs and the fascists, the suspension of asylum claims.

Then, overwhelmed and terrified by too much reality, I would turn my attention toward more occult attempts to make sense of the world. I taught myself to read tarot (why not?), studied astrology, even attempted to communicate with the hummingbirds nesting outside my window.

In bed, between bouts of fever, I read *The Oracle*, William J. Broad's 2007 book about Delphi, that centuries-old stop along the Greek tourist trail built long ago for those in search of what the fates held in store. I understand now that I'd picked up the book seeking both a return to Greece and a framework for divination: a way to know the unknowable and increasingly terrifying future.

"The Oracle," writes Broad, "was simply a lamp awaiting divine illumination."

. . .

Ben and I had visited Delphi the previous summer, and reading Broad's book was a portal back to that time, now suddenly and forever a distinct *before.*

We'd awoken at sunrise in Athens one morning and tumbled into our rental car, leaving the clogged city and emerging rather quickly into the sparse, dry wilds to the north, where the cicadas clicked and grasses made their arid music with the wind. The road coiled its way up toward Mount Parnassus—a bare, gleaming cliff that seemed to plunge directly to the center of the earth.

It was said in ancient texts that Apollo—"the god of light and order, reason and prophecy"—went wandering through the mountains in search of a home. He settled upon Mount Parnassus, that great dome of rock where springs burbled from the hillsides and vapors emerged from a mysterious cleft as if in divine exhalation. "In this place," says the god in the Homeric "Hymn to Apollo," "I am minded to build a glorious temple to be an oracle for men." But first he had to kill the serpentine beast that ruled the cleft—a victory, writes Broad in *The Oracle,* that "came to symbolize the god's victory over the powers of darkness."

A temple was built where the vapors rose. A small, rounded stone called the *omphalos,* or navel, marked off the innermost chambers where, for over a thousand years, a succession of priestesses, each chosen by the Delphic council for her chastity and good manners, made their sacred connection with Apollo in order to receive prophecy. Once a month, for nine months of the year, the presiding priestess would wake with the dawn, bathe in the sacred springs, and enter the temple's central chamber. Inside, according to the writings of Plutarch, she would hear questions from the pilgrims who came in droves to seek guidance from the oracle. Sitting on a three-legged stool surrounded by laurel leaves, she would inhale the pneuma, then merge, via trance, with Apollo. When she surfaced she'd have an answer, often swaddled in enigma.

The oracle was available to everyone (though the rich could skip the lines). Kings, military leaders, and commoners came from far and near to seek counsel there. They asked about infertility, whom to marry, when to plant, how to mediate disputes, whether and when to go into battle. Evidence suggests, writes Broad, that Delphic guidance "repeatedly changed the course of history."

As Ben and I wound our way to the remains of Delphi, I understood that I, too, was a pilgrim in search of answers. I was excavating the past and the present in search of an alternative route, and I was looking beyond the material world to help me find it.

We parked alongside buses crammed with tourists, then queued up amid a stifling throng. The museum was all facts and dates and stone—no heart, no spirit. We tramped alongside the crowds up the Sacred Way, a dirt path surrounded by the sun-bleached ruins of monuments. What kind of portal to the divine was this?

At the top of the hill, Ben and I found a shaded bench where I lay down for a rest. Before I knew it, I fell into a deep, untroubled sleep, the kind that had been eluding me for days.

When I woke—I'd slept for nearly an hour—Ben and I found a nearby spring that Ben's mother had told us about, a place she remembered from a visit when she was a girl. The water plunged from the hillside in an abundant stream, just as she'd recalled, and we recorded the sound to send to her thousands of miles away. "Greeks saw enchanted waters as able to cure disease, inspire poetry, and—most especially—induce raptures conductive to augury," writes Broad. It certainly soothed us, all that water spilling from deep inside the earth. I liked knowing that the sounds were securely stored on my phone now—that at any time in the future, I could listen to the springs at Delphi as a reminder of the long journeys humans undertake because there is something they believe in at the end.

The oracle fell, as did animistic traditions the world over, at the hands of Christianity. *Tell the king, the fair-wrought house has fallen. . . . The fountains now are silent; the voice is stilled.* By the fourth century CE, "Delphi was pillaged, destroyed and then forgotten," writes Broad. The people built Christian churches; then came earthquakes and avalanches and the passage of time. All was quiet and buried until the late seventeenth century, when the site of the oracle was rediscovered by explorers. After a long fight, the French won the bid to excavate the site toward the end of the nineteenth century. By then, spiritualism had caught fire in Europe, partly in response to the industrial age and the mannered sensibilities of the Victorian era. What mysteries did the uncovering of the oracle have in store? "The world of arts and letters," writes Broad, "shivered with anticipation." Like me, they were hungry for both meaning and magic.

But the results were disappointing. The French could find no archaeological evidence of a crack in the earth or the existence of pneuma. They dubbed the oracle a fraud, an elaborate deception, Plutarch and the lineage of ancient priestesses either lunatics or sellers of snake oil.

The oracle as sham became the reigning truth for nearly a century. Then, Broad explains, archaeologist John R. Hale teamed up with geologist Jelle Zeilinga de Boer to discover that the site of the Delphic Oracle had been built directly atop the intersection of two major fault lines, in one of the most seismically active regions on earth. They found that vapors containing ethylene, a sweet-smelling chemical capable of inducing a euphoric trance, likely rose right into the heart of the temple. With this discovery, the legacy and meaning of Delphi shifted in academic and popular perception yet again. Plutarch's writings had been true, after all—for what is considered "true" seems always to be changing.

But what about the prophecies, all those times the oracle managed to light the way forward? Broad offers that science, as ever, could do little to explain the divine.

When I awoke at the top of the hill, it occurred to me in my hot haze that an oracle is merely a mechanism of divine orientation, a map. At the heart of any search for truth—including what I sought as a journalist, what propelled me forward from that first trip to Greece onward—was an attempt to look things in the face, to become un-lost.

19.

It didn't require divine prophecy to predict the outcome of the criminal case against the Moria 6. In March 2021, the two defendants whom the government recognized as minors stood trial for arson and membership in a criminal group. The trial lasted seven hours, and the judges deliberated for just ten minutes before sentencing them each to five years in prison. The other four would be tried later that summer as adults, even though Ali and two of his codefendants claimed to be minors—and now had the paperwork from Afghanistan to prove it.

International borders remained closed due to COVID. I continued to follow the case from afar: via press releases, twitter feeds, communication with activists and the legal team. The fire, it was becoming clear, was intimately connected to the questions at the heart of much of my writing—in this book, and in other projects, too: the costs of borders; the scapegoats of national identity; who is afforded a sense of belonging, and how.

The June trial took place on the island of Chios, some two hours south of Lesbos by ferry. Chios, which had also received a large number of refugees over the years, was chosen in an effort at judge and juror neutrality, and to avoid protests or other such disruptions. The location also made it difficult for some witnesses to make the trial. Of the thirty witnesses called, only fifteen showed up.

Later, Ali and his attorneys would, as if conducting an archaeological investigation, patiently piece together the events of the trial for me to assemble into a story.

A few days before the trial, Ali and his codefendants were brought to Chios, where they were kept in a small temporary jail facility near the main harbor rather than in the larger adult prison outside town. They were, if unlucky in perhaps every other way, incredibly fortunate to have landed the attorneys they did—and Ali knew as much. During their months of waiting in prison, it had become clear that the government was furnishing little evidence against him and his codefendants, yet the two registered minors had been convicted all the same. These lawyers were their only hope.

There was Effie Doussi, an independent attorney working on the case, who was from the Peloponnese region. After completing her legal training on the mainland, she had moved to Lesbos to use her skills in support of the arriving refugees. She worked long hours to file asylum claims and appeals, apply for family reunification in other EU countries, and, increasingly over the years, help refugees fight criminal charges brought against them. A tall woman with short hair and angular glasses who had a habit of bringing the palms of her hands to her forehead as if in disbelief at the very story she was telling me, Effie spoke partly in the parlance of humanitarian outrage and partly in poetry. (*"It's not a matter of leniency; I love others, and thus remain human."*) Just a few years into the work, she had sensed burnout nearing, brought on by fighting a system that seemed to keep changing the rules to stack them against her clients, even when their cases were strong and deserving. But she hadn't been able to say no to the six young men accused of lighting Moria on fire.

Another member of the team, Natasha Dailiani, was a founding attorney of Legal Centre Lesvos, which had had taken on the cases of the

Moria 6. Dailiani, with her bright eyes and brighter countenance, had gotten into this line of work out of a deep belief that everyone is vulnerable and worthy of protection. The work wore on her as well. One of her first big cases was particularly upsetting: in 2017, thirty-five refugees peacefully protesting conditions in Moria—most of them from sub-Saharan Africa—were brutally beaten by police and then, perversely, arrested for assault. One day, many months pregnant, Dailiani went to visit them in prison. "When you're pregnant," she would tell me, "you see everyone as a child." It was clear how much her visit lifted the spirits of her clients—in spite of all they were up against, in spite of how powerless she often felt in the face of the forces working against them.

And here she was again, years later, working on yet another case rooted in the injustice of Moria, feeling as if she was the only hope for another group of young men in prison. In the case of the Moria 6, though, she was able to marshal considerable optimism. The government had a weak case, and she was certain her clients were innocent. In spite of the country's hostility to migrants, she felt her team had a good chance of winning in court.

But Natasha's colleague Vicky Angelidou told her and the others not to get their hopes up. Vicky was a seasoned criminal justice attorney from Athens, with a spider tattoo on her hand that flashed when she lit a cigarette or lifted a pen. She was older than the others, more jaded, and she knew that the prospects for the defendants weren't so good. "It was a predetermined case," she would tell me later. This was something she'd known all along.

The defense team also arrived on Chios by ferry a few days before the trial, with Natasha's toddler in tow. As they disembarked, the police ordered the group aside and began searching their belongings without explanation. This rattled the attorneys, which seemed to be the point. The next morning, Effie and Vicky headed to the jail to meet with Ali and the three others. The attending police officer greeted the lawyers with an apology; because of COVID measures, they didn't have their usual room available for the attorneys to meet with their clients. Instead, they were let into a cell adjacent to the one where the accused were sleeping. It seemed not to have been cleaned in ages: crumbs, bits of eggshells, and other trash covered the concrete bed frames, the only place for them to sit.

When Ali and the others were brought in, they greeted the attorneys, and, upon seeing the mess, quickly went back to their cell to fetch their bedsheets, which they laid down so the attorneys could sit somewhere clean. This detail—the care and attention these young men were paying to the comfort of their attorneys—struck the team. Each would later mention this moment to me—the ones who had been there, the ones who had merely heard the story secondhand. It was a sign, as Effie Doussi put it, that these young people had maintained their humanity in spite of the injustice and indignities of their circumstances.

At 8:30 a.m. on Friday, June 11, the court was called to order. But before the trial could officially begin, there were some housekeeping items to attend to. Out of COVID concerns, one judge announced, no extra people would be allowed in court—no independent international observers, as is customary in such cases, and no journalists. Everyone in the courtroom was asked to introduce themselves and state their affiliation; if they weren't part of the defense team or the prosecution, they were instructed to leave. Even a representative of the United Nations High Commissioner for Refugees, which often sent delegates to observe criminal court cases involving refugees around the world, was instructed to leave. In the end, only the three judges, the jury members, the defense team, the prosecutors, an interpreter, and the four defendants—along with seven police officers—were allowed to remain. Seven police officers to monitor only fifteen others seemed like overkill to the defense, and if COVID was really the main concern, it was a risk in and of itself. They were convinced that the government wanted a closed trial and was using COVID as an excuse. But there was no arguing the point. The courtroom was cleared, and the trial began.

The defense immediately lodged an objection of basic admissibility. Three of the four defendants were minors, they claimed, and shouldn't be in this courtroom in the first place. They again furnished their clients' original documents from Afghanistan, which clearly stated their dates of birth. But their Greek paperwork said otherwise: Ali said this was because he had been disbelieved by the authorities when he landed on Lesbos, and the other two claimed to have lied to the border authorities and UNHCR, declaring they were older than they were. (Misrepresenting one's age is a not entirely uncommon practice among refugees, depending on the myths to which they subscribe: unaccompanied minors often believe that if they admit to being minors arriving without family, they will be deported home. And adults sometimes claim to be minors in the belief that it will get them greater protection and a better prospect of asylum.)

The prosecution had taken X-rays of the young men's wrists and had them evaluated by a social scientist with a criminology and anthropology background, who deemed them to be evidence that the three were over the age of eighteen. But criminal anthropologists were not doctors, the defense argued—and the prosecution's expert had not employed the methodology used by the Ministry of Migration, which followed the guidelines recommended by the European Union's asylum support office. Citing the confidentiality of health records, the prosecution had also denied the defense attorneys' requests for the X-rays so they could conduct an independent analysis. But when the defendants had asked to access their own X-rays, their requests were also denied.

In the end, the judges held that not enough evidence had been furnished to prove that the defendants were minors. The trial would proceed.

The defense was left to argue the case based on the facts—which, on the face of it, should not have been too hard, given how little evidence there was against the defendants. But the case wasn't being waged purely on the facts. Like most of the rising number of other criminal cases being lodged against refugees in Greece, it was political in nature. In December 2020, for instance, a Somali man named Hanad Abdi Mohammad boarded a boat to make safe passage to Greece. When a storm hit, he took the helm to save himself and his fellow passengers from drowning. For this, he was arrested for human smuggling and slapped with the absurd sentence of 142 years. This was not an isolated case. Pinning human-smuggling charges on migrants was becoming a more common tactic in Greece, even though the fact that Turkish smuggling rings force migrants to pilot the boats is well known. The Greek authorities were finding other ways to prosecute refugees, too. In a particularly grisly example, a father was arrested and charged with child endangerment after his two-year-old drowned in a shipwreck off the coast of Samos island. He faced up to ten years in prison.

It was no wonder, then, that Vicky doubted that the defendants would have a fair day in court.

Still, the government's case was shoddy. The defense team recounted that the prosecutors played a low-quality cell phone video showing a group of young men stoking the flames in Moria—but the video was taken from behind, and there was no way to positively identify the people in the video, or to prove that they alone had started the fire that burned the whole camp down.

There was, however, an eyewitness who claimed to have seen each of the Moria 6 light the fires. His account was central to the prosecution's case. This man—an Afghan elder, a Pashtun, of a different ethnic group from the Moria 6, most of whom were Hazara—had tipped off the police in Lesbos, and this had led to the arrests. But the eyewitness didn't appear in court in Chios that day, for he and his family were now nowhere to be found. No one from the prosecutor's office or the Ministry of Migration knew where they had gone, and the defense hadn't been able to find him, either. He and his family had been granted asylum shortly after he gave his testimony to the police and had been allowed to transfer off Lesbos at a time when, for COVID restrictions, even Greeks had to get special permission to leave. After that, he seemed to have absconded into the ether.

As the witness was not there to offer his testimony in person, one of the defense lawyers argued to the court that his written statement should be deemed inadmissible. She reminded the judges that there was precedent for this—in this very courtroom, in fact. In another Moria arson case two years earlier, the prosecutor himself had dropped the case when the sole witness who was to testify as to the defendant's guilt couldn't be located during the trial. Now the defense argued that the testimony the witness had already provided was not reliable, and was suspicious enough to seem perhaps even the product of a quid pro quo arrangement. The judges, though, appeared to have no intention of dropping this case, and they allowed the prosecution to read the testimony into the record.

The testimony itself lacked much detail. The witness had provided only the first names of the accused, for one thing—names that, in the Afghan community, were quite common. He said he had seen six boys start the fire in Zone 9 on the night of September 8—but according to the fire report, Zone 9 didn't burn until September 9 and was deemed to have caught on fire as a result of the wind. Plus, none of the minors even lived in the zone that he said he saw being lit on fire.

Later, the prosecution called the fire chief to the stand. He testified that the fire began in another zone entirely. When cross-examined by the defense, who pointed to the fire report, he corrected himself: the fire had actually begun elsewhere, he said. Had he been coached, the defense wondered, or had he just made an honest mistake?

The trial adjourned for the day, with an exhausted, deflated defense team heading back to their hotel. Still, some of them held out hope.

When court resumed session on the second day, the defense team focused on the issue of mitigating circumstances. Notwithstanding that the four defendants and their lawyers maintained their innocence, should the court find them guilty, the defense team believed, they must take the inhumane conditions of Moria into account when weighing their punishment. To testify about the horrific state of the camp, they brought in several witnesses and international experts. But as all of the defense attorneys recollected to me, one of the judges kept interrupting this testimony. Of course Moria was a horrible place, he said, but he didn't see the relevance of this line of argument.

Every argument the defense made, it seemed, was being rejected, every objection overruled. They felt the judges were siding with the prosecution on every count.

"We felt alone," Natasha told me.

And Ali? Throughout the trial, he and his codefendants had little idea what was going on. The court had hired an interpreter, but the judges failed to allow sufficient pauses for more than short summaries of what was being said, despite the repeated requests by the defense attorneys. The young men didn't protest. They had put all their trust in their lawyers, who at this point were their only hope. But although Ali did not doubt that the attorneys were working hard on their behalf, he could tell things weren't looking good.

Late in the afternoon on June 12, the verdict was issued: the four defendants tried as adults were found guilty and sentenced to ten years in prison. Before the interpreter could even repeat the verdict in Dari, the defendants could see it in their lawyers' fallen faces.

"I couldn't look them in the eyes," Effie Doussi recalled. "I wanted the earth to open up and swallow me."

Immediately, Ali and his codefendants thanked their lawyers for trying. That was gutting to the attorneys.

The police rounded up the young men, cuffed them, and led them outside. Their lawyers followed. A small crowd of supporters awaited them on the street. As they were being loaded into the police vehicles, the defendants could hear their supporters shouting—"like a beautiful symphony," Doussi would later tell me—"*Azadi, azadi,*" the Dari word for "freedom." From there, the convicts were taken to prison on the mainland, where, along with the two previously convicted as minors, they would serve their sentences.

20.

A few months before the Chios trial, Greece had announced it would open back up to visitors from abroad. The Greek economy had lost millions during the year of halted global tourism, and the government was determined to make the country a premier destination for the first postvaccination summer. "All You Want Is Greece," went the clunky slogan adopted to lure tourists back. I booked a flight and happened to arrive soon after the Moria verdict was issued.

I spent my first morning back in Greece wandering around in the thick heat, attempting to stave off my jet lag. Within an hour, I was back at the Little Metropolis Church. I hadn't been looking for it but was delighted to have found it again—as if a sign of rightful return. Of course there would be no quacking duck this time, I knew, no austere duck mother, but I kept my eyes peeled all the same. I admired the somber frescoes inside the church, put a coin in the collection box, and lit a candle for the future.

The next day, I met up with my friend Melissa and headed to the Acropolis. The place was packed once again with travelers from all around the world, looking backward in time. All we wanted was Greece! The ruins were strewn with the accoutrements of restoration: rickety scaffolding, corrugated metal storage facilities, looming cranes. *Don't touch the marble*, read sign after sign. Melissa pulled out her camera, but it was hardly possible to take a photograph of the ruins that didn't include some encroachment of the new machinery designed to maintain a particular version of the old and to keep it from further decay. Perhaps such a photo is not unlike the Acropolis ruins themselves: a futile attempt at purity—of the past, undisturbed.

From the Parthenon we made our way on foot to Anafiotika, that whitewashed neighborhood—not to get lost, as Ben and I had, but to look for Demetrios, the old man on the hillside. Back in California, I'd thought about him from time to time. Had he survived the plague? Had his politics hardened or shifted? Had he been a mere apparition—as I wondered about the duck mother, the possessed donkey who'd taken hold of Ben's arm, and the spiders on Hydra?

We wandered for about an hour, the small pathways twisting up and down the hillsides among the empty white houses with their pots of bright flowers. All was quiet. The day grew hotter, and we grew hungry. After a while it was clear we wouldn't find him. It was a silly idea even to have tried, as if everything from before had been pinned in place like butterfly specimens, just waiting for me. We turned in search of breakfast.

But as we descended the hill, I heard it: a soft bouzouki strumming. I looked at Melissa with wide eyes, and we walked in the direction of the music. There he was with his instrument. This time, instead of a hat he wore a plastic face shield, and instead of coffee he sipped tsipouro, a Greek brandy, though it was still morning.

"Demetrios?" I said.

"Ah, you know me!" he replied happily, and he motioned for us to take a seat as he resumed the song. Another tourist was perched on a step next to him, bobbing her head to the rhythm.

When he finished, he turned to me and said again, "You know me!" I told him I remembered him from another trip, two years before. He nodded, seeming none too surprised. I asked if he came here every day.

"Every day, every day," he said. Even during COVID, when the tourists didn't come, he came. He came to sing.

I asked about the birds. Oh, the birds. They didn't fly too close anymore, he explained, on account of the cats. He riffled around in his instrument case and pulled out a handful of kibble, which he cast onto the stones. Three mewling cats emerged from the shadows, snatched up the food, and dashed into the brush.

"Where are you from?" he asked Melissa and me, and we told him. He picked up his bouzouki again and began to play "The Star-Spangled Banner"—"Just for you," he said. After playing a few bars and securing our laughter, he said, "Okay, Greek music now!" and began to sing a rebetiko.

Rebetiko is the determined, percussive music, simultaneously gay and mournful, that features the bouzouki and is now considered quintessentially Greek. But in fact, the bouzouki is the descendant of the Turkish buzuq and related to the Byzantine tambouras—instruments decidedly Eastern in their provenance and timbre. After the 1922 Catastrophe, the Asia Minor Greeks brought this instrument with them from their former homes. At the time, the Greek people were split in their response to these refugees from the East and the customs they carried. Yes, these newcomers spoke Greek and were Orthodox, but were they to be trusted? They were, after all, from Türkiye. ("*Turko!*" Evanthia would yell at my father and her other grandchildren anytime they misbehaved.)

In the decade after the Catastrophe, a strongman named Ioannis Metaxas rose to power in Greece. His goal was to rebuild the nation-state and create a "Third Greek Civilization" aligned with what he saw as western European values—to become, in effect, western European in image and in deed. But enacting this revisionist revival of Greece would require curating and controlling information, and at the same time sanitizing Greek arts and culture according to his nationalistic vision.

"I forbid any of you," he proclaimed to university students in Salonica, now Thessaloniki, "male or female, to have any ideas other than those of the State. I require you not only to have the same ideas as the State, but to believe in them and to work accordingly with enthusiasm. If any of you have different ideas, he or she had better not be educated."

Right away Metaxas opened an office with the sinister title of "Undersecretariat of Press and Tourism," which was created in the explicit image of Joseph Goebbels's surveillance system in Berlin. This office oversaw all media in Greek territory, from lectures to advertising to radio broadcasts to plays. Tourism would be critical to Metaxas's project, for modern Greece's national identity was determined, in large part, by how it was seen and how it wanted to be seen by outsiders.

The bouzouki was a problem in the eyes of the Undersecretariat, coming as it did from "the East" and serving as a reminder of a long history of multiethnic Greek identity. In the preceding years, the instrument had become a staple of what historian Roderick Beaton calls "the urban underclass" of Greece, destitute types who, in both stereotype and action, drifted into a "world of petty crime" and "defiantly antisocial society"—a class that included many of the Asia Minor refugees from the 1920s. Their rebetika sang of crime and love, of uprising and outlaws, of the lost homeland and a lost past—songs that, as Beaton put it, "celebrated a different kind of self-sufficiency from the official one."

Naturally, the rebetika had to be banned, and the bouzouki along with it. "Instruments were liable to be seized and smashed, their owners taken in for questioning," Beaton writes. The baglamas, a smaller, bouzouki-like instrument, became popular because it was easier to hide.

In spite of the attempts to suppress the rebetika, the music flourished and made its way from the lawless underclasses into the mainstream. And in spite of the music's provenance, the sounds of the bouzouki gradually became the sound of Greece itself, and the rebetika anthems of Greek pride. It's this music that one hears in the tavernas, in the cafés, strummed by buskers like Demetrios in the streets. The bouzouki was even incorporated into the flashy, tourist-luring videos created for the "All You Want Is Greece" campaign.

And it had worked. The tourists were back; Demetrios had his audience again, the rebetika played on as if it had never not been and never stopped.

All cities, Svetlana Boym claims, are largely porous. They lack an absolute identity, instead "reflecting the layers of time and history, social problems, as well as ingenious techniques of urban survival." Yet, she writes, travelers to foreign cities often mistake this porosity for "a picturesque vision of authenticity."

It was time to go. I plucked some euros from my wallet and dropped them in Demetrios's instrument case near the bag of kibble, wishing him well.

"Lauren-moo!" he called as we walked away. By now the cats had settled in around him. He lifted his bouzouki. "Come back and see me again! I will be here!"

21.

From Athens we boarded the train to Thessaloniki, Greece's second-largest city, up near the contested border with the Republic of North Macedonia ("a fake country," a Bulgarian friend likes to say—but what is it that makes a country "real"?). I scrolled the news as the train slid through the landscape—miles and miles of sunflowers. The air outside our window was hazy, for that very day a wildfire had erupted to our south. Given the wind and the dry heat, much of the entire country was under a fire warning. I studied the map of the quickening blaze: red regions that were on fire, orange and yellow regions of high and moderate risk, and green regions where things were still safe. The train sped north toward the green zone, as if trying to outrun it all.

Melissa stayed in Thessaloniki while I rented a car and drove farther east through swaths of industry that gave way to mountainous expanses until, after a few hours, I reached the border with Türkiye. This was one of the most militarized borders in Europe. Because of COVID and bilateral tensions, the border was closed to travelers; only commercial vehicles were allowed to cross. Trucks idled for miles on the Greek side of the checkpoint, waiting to be let through. As in Norway—as in Mexico, Texas, El Salvador, Uganda, Kenya, Thailand, Brazil—I had the urge to stand at the border and look at it for a while.

In truth, I knew little of the politics of this particular border then; to me, it appeared a sleepy outpost, little more. The border town of Feres was sealed up and quiet: empty tavernas, empty shops, blinds drawn on so many windows. The Evros River carved the border here, just to the east of the ghostly town. I found a shortcut on Google Maps that would lead me to its banks. The route twisted along a paved road until it turned sharply uphill, becoming dirt. I followed the little blue way-finding dot on my phone's map faithfully, but with each passing meter the road became rougher and more vague. The car bounced wildly on the uneven surface, and scrub scraped against the undercarriage. My phone pinged a warning: I had only 5 percent of my battery power left. My charger, it appeared, had stopped working. Without any other map, I found myself once again becoming lost.

By now the road was mere rocks. I rounded a sharp bend, and there in front of me was an elderly shepherd with a leathered face, knee-high boots, and a tall wooden staff, surrounded by roughly a hundred goats. Relieved to have encountered another human in this desolate stretch, I waved merrily, but he just shook his head in exasperation and shooed me on. By the next bend, the evidence was undeniable: this supposed road was a sham. My map had erred and, as the shepherd saw quite well, I had no business making my way here in my red two-door sedan. Defeated, I turned the car around. I dreaded encountering the shepherd again. But when I returned to where I'd passed him not five minutes before, he was gone—vanished. Not a goat in sight.

I lurched back to the main road, then headed east again toward the official checkpoint, following the signs in Greek and Turkish rather than my dying phone. I would later learn how lucky I had been that the road and my map had failed me, for the entire river is a militarized zone and had I crossed into it, as the shepherd likely knew, I would have been swiftly detained, perhaps even arrested and charged. Back on the highway, military jeeps and cargo trucks packed with soldiers roared on all sides of me, defending the outer reaches of the EU. Refugees who crossed here today—as people had crossed since long before it was a border—were often captured by Greek border guards, held in detention, and sometimes tortured and beaten before being marched back across the river into Türkiye, as if to deter them from trying again. The press had even documented the Greek authorities covertly depositing refugees on small islands in the middle of the river, where, stuck without a boat, some died from exposure or lack of access to medical care. But none of those journalists would be so foolish as to step right up to the line, as I had nearly done.

These so-called pushbacks of refugees are against both international and domestic law. In legal terms, a pushback is refoulement—a dirty word in international law, for a signatory to the UN Refugee Convention cannot legally expel a person asking for safe harbor before they've had a chance to plead their case. And yet pushbacks were now happening in Greece—and elsewhere, too—with near impunity, on both land and sea. Greek Coast Guard vessels frequently stopped boats in the Aegean, destroyed their engines, and dragged them back to Turkish waters to drift, and sometimes to sink. Increasingly, authorities were even removing people who had already landed on the Greek islands and depositing them in flimsy life rafts on the Turkish side of the sea border. "No pushbacks, no pushbacks!" the new arrivals shout to anyone who comes upon them in hiding—for most already know that the Greek authorities will covertly try to send them back. So when their boats land, refugees scramble to shore and into the woods, where they call international rescue lines and appeal for help from the United Nations. But rarely does anyone come to their aid anymore. Instead, in a horrific game of cat and mouse, the new arrivals try to make their way to the nearest refugee camp—sometimes hundreds of kilometers from where they landed—and officially register their presence before the Greek authorities can find them. Once a person is registered, it's much more difficult for them to be disappeared.

Pushbacks have been documented since the 1980s, but the Greek government now seems to be employing them as a matter of policy, though officials deny they are happening at all. Leaked documents reveal that officials within the EU border authority, Frontex, are aware of the widespread pushbacks—and that Frontex boats may have even helped to facilitate them in some cases. Because they are undertaken covertly, exact numbers are hard to come by, but in 2020, a sea watch organization, Mare Liberum (which has since disbanded, in part because of intimidation from the Greek government), documented 9,798 individuals pushed back into the Aegean. In 2021, a single NGO had received reports from more than 15,000 individuals forcibly returned across the border. People were found dead in Evros, dead on the islands in the middle of the river, dead and drowned out at sea. But whether they were found dead or alive, officials made no formal record of these arrivals, as if these people had never existed.

Greece is not alone in this practice. The Australian navy has turned boats bearing asylum seekers back to Indonesia and Sri Lanka or forced them onto neighboring islands instead of letting them land on Australian shores. Thai authorities have dragged rickety crafts packed with asylum seekers out to sea, sometimes to their deaths. In 2021, Polish militias beat refugees back across the border to Belarus, where families froze to death in the forest as they tried to cross into Europe. And at its southern border, the US government used COVID-19 threats and an obscure part of a public health law called Title 42 to return asylum seekers to Mexico. While I was reporting in Greece, a photo of a US Border Patrol agent on horseback chasing down Haitian asylum seekers in Texas ricocheted across the internet. People were, rightfully, outraged. This was an image of pushbacks in action, dressed up as law.

These illegal expulsions seem an increasingly common strategy in a world where more people are on the move with each passing year, and where inequality, climate change, totalitarian persecution, and war—the forces that uproot people from home—show no signs of subsiding. But unlike other callous deterrence strategies like border walls, family separation, and inhumane detention, pushbacks tend to work. In Greece, fewer people were attempting the crossing because they knew the risk of being illegally returned was high, and thus were finding other routes instead. It was the efficacy of the pushbacks that was perhaps most alarming of all.

I didn't see evidence of this brutal border handiwork that day in Evros, nor was it likely that I would any other day, for such actions are deliberately hidden from view. But all the patrolling army cars and police vehicles hinted at the existence of this clandestine world of refoulement. They reminded me, too, of all the days I'd spent in South Texas, where the US Border Patrol trucks scour the sparse terrain.

I parked my car on a side road near the idling trucks, next to a small shack advertising olives and honey. Melissa was a baker, and I wanted to bring a jar of honey back for her. Melissa: her name means "bee" in Greek, and *meli* means "honey." The man behind the counter wrapped a jar of meli for me in plastic as the trucks inched slowly forward in their interminable eastbound line. Borderless honey, made by bees that sipped freely from flowers on either side.

22.

I drove back to Thessaloniki that day, and soon after, Melissa and I flew to Lesbos, where, I thought, I'd be able to get to the bottom of what actually happened in Moria.

I began by interviewing anyone who would speak to me, trying to fill in the holes: dozens upon dozens of refugees who had been there the night of the fire; medical interpreters; NGO workers; attorneys; activists and volunteers. I met with politicians, Moria townspeople, human rights researchers.

No one I spoke to outside the government believed the Moria 6 were to blame, but the government officials were steadfast: the men's guilt had been established, and it was a closed case now. I began to realize that not only would I not be able to figure out who started the fire; I wouldn't even be able to prove that the Moria 6 hadn't lit it, not with any certainty. Memories of that night were abundant, but official documents eluded me. I asked Kostas Moutzouris, the right-wing regional governor of the North Aegean, about the fire report. "You won't find it," he told me. It was sealed; he himself hadn't seen it. When I asked the minister of migration about the Moria fire, he declined to speak about the case, claiming that it was really a matter for the criminal justice system. Fair enough. But the prosecution, the fire department, and the police all declined to speak with me as well, or to furnish me with information. Trial evidence was confidential, and if the defense shared it with me, they risked government retribution. It was proving impossible to gain access to almost anything upon which the prosecution's case had been built.

The very elements that made the story a matter of public concern—the differing versions of events, the obscuring of facts, the thin evidence, and the mockery of a trial—were the things that made it a thorny one to tell according to the conventions of journalism. The conventions of journalism, it seemed to me, were in this case a snake eating its own tail.

There was also a troubling irony of the Moria fire case: just how many people were happy the camp was finally gone. Because of the fire, thousands of refugees had ultimately made it to mainland Greece, or to better-resourced European countries, and though the new camp was far from perfect and access was highly restricted, most felt that it was, indeed, better than Moria. Many locals, too, saw Moria's destruction as a move in a positive direction—at least at first. As Vaselis the baker had said, "Moria camp burning was a gift from God."

Governor Moutzouris told me, "It is tragic to say that the fire helped, but it helped. In a certain way, it was very successful." The number of refugees on the island was far lower now. "If they are really guilty, I am happy," he told me of the conviction of the Moria 6. "Tragic, tragic. Although they helped us. They helped the local society."

When I met with representatives from UNHCR in their plush, air-conditioned offices, I asked what paperwork they could share with me. What I wanted most was access to the fire report. They didn't have it, they told me. Nor did they have copies of the indictment or any other documents related to the burning of the camp. They did, however, offer me a colored map of Moria printed some weeks before it burned, on a piece of paper so big I had to fold it in quarters to fit it in my notebook. During each interview that followed, I pulled out the map and spread it on the table so people could trace it with their fingers as they recalled the night of the fire and its aftermath. But each of them seemed to use the map to tell a slightly different story.

One afternoon I drove to the remains of Moria camp and walked among the ghostly wreckage, trying to find the landmarks I remembered from when Thi and I had visited two years before. Carcasses of a few buildings remained, and the odd tent had survived, but most of Moria was leveled into a thick, charred carpet of clothing scraps, shards of kitchen items, and broken toys. Sheep had taken up residence in the old camp chapel; when I poked my head in, they spooked and took off running, spooking me in turn. The *Welcome to Europe, Human Rights Graveyard* graffiti marked what was once the camp's front entrance—the graffiti, too, written as both a matter of fact and an oracle.

When I made my way through the ruins, I began to smell fire—not the charred ruins, but actual, live flames. I looked around and noticed a small group of people sitting beneath a wide-canopied tree that had somehow survived the blaze, inside what had been the walled Reception and Identification Center. From their dress and the headscarves the women wore, I sensed they were refugees. They spotted me and waved me over. As I neared, I saw that they had built a cook fire on the edges of a concrete foundation, where they were boiling water for tea and preparing a picnic. The two older women introduced themselves and motioned for me to sit down with their families—three teenagers, a young girl, and a man in his twenties—who had formed a circle around a metal platter of fruits and nuts.

They were from Afghanistan and they had all lived in Moria for over a year, they told me, save for the young man, who was just visiting Lesbos for a few days. This was the first time any of them had been back since the fire. In the new camp they were allowed to exit for only a few hours a week, and today, their designated release day, they'd decided to pool their money for a taxi to come here and see what remained.

"I hated it here," said Sedique, one of the teenagers, in English. "But also, we were so curious to know what it was like now, what had happened."

"It was a bad home," Fatimah, another of the teenagers said, "but it was home." She poured me a cup of tea.

Today was a special occasion because of the young man's visit—Mehdi was his name. He sat across the circle from a beaming Sedique, working hard to make her and everyone else laugh. Later, Sedique would tell me the story of how she'd met him. A year before, sitting outside her tent at Moria, she'd heard one of her friends chattering about a cousin of hers in Germany who was looking for a girlfriend. The friend showed Sedique a picture of Mehdi on her phone. He was handsome, and since she didn't have much else to do in Moria, she agreed to talk to him. They began texting via WhatsApp and then speaking regularly in the mornings and evenings. She liked him. He was funny, he was studying at a German university, and he held feminist beliefs—including that Sedique should finish her studies before she got married or had kids. Eventually Sedique's parents sanctioned the relationship. Now he'd come to Lesbos to formally ask for her hand.

As we sipped our tea, the group told me their own versions of what had happened the night the camp burned, how they'd had to take to the streets, on the run yet again. They hadn't heard about the Moria 6 trial and the convictions. Most refugees I spoke to in Lesbos hadn't. In a way, this made sense. Former residents of Moria had been scattered from Lesbos after the fire—some had been transferred to the mainland, others had been offered status in other European countries, still others had been deported or had snuck out in the bellies of trucks that loaded onto the Athens-bound ferries. Plus, the names and images of the Moria 6 had been kept out of the papers to protect their identities. There was no way for people to notice that these particular young men were gone. They could have been anywhere. Like the victims of pushbacks, they had become ghosts.

The picnickers were disappointed to hear that their fellow countrymen—and such young ones at that—were in prison for burning down Moria. They were dissatisfied with the official story as well. Motioning to the acres upon acres of scorched land and echoing what so many others had already told me, Sedique said, "Look, Moria is so big. Six people cannot burn this whole place alone."

Later that afternoon, I drove to the north of the island to visit the elders in Sappho's garden in Klio again.

"Koukla!" Annula greeted me, offering a hug. I was so happy to see them again, as I might feel seeing family. We drank coffee and ate sweets while my hosts talked about olden times, and about recent events, too. Fewer refugees were making it to land anymore, they knew. Fewer refugees came through town on their way to Moria, so many kilometers away—Annula remembered one in a headscarf, trying to pay for a loaf of bread with a two-hundred-euro note, having no idea how much the bill was worth; she'd bought the woman the bread and told her to keep her money.

COVID had something to do with the decreased arrivals, they suspected, but also the business with the Coast Guard stopping people at sea or kicking them out once they'd already reached shore. It was a tragedy what was happening, they felt. Forced migration is always a tragedy.

And the fire, too, was tragic—though it seemed almost inevitable that a place like Moria would be turned to ruin sooner or later.

Annula had a story she'd forgotten to tell me the last time I'd come, a story about a key. The key was a large one, cast in an old foundry, and it unlocked the door to her grandparents' house in Asia Minor. Her grandmother had taken it with her when she fled in 1922, perhaps out of habit (one leaves the house with one's keys, after all) or perhaps from wishful thinking—that one day she'd return. The key had been passed down through the generations and now sat in a special box in Annula's home.

A few years earlier, Annula signed up for a tour to visit the Turkish port of İzmir, as Smyrna was now called, a roughly four-hour ferry ride across the Aegean from Lesbos. She'd taken the key with her, hopeful she could find a way to visit the town her family had come from and locate their old home by trying the key in all the doors. But unfortunately, she told me with some degree of sorrow, the tour was on a strict schedule and couldn't deviate from their itinerary. She'd traveled all that way, key secured in her pocketbook, but hadn't found its door. No matter, she said, shaking off the memory. One day she'd go back to locate the home that, had it not been for war and displacement, would still belong to her family today.

We sipped our coffee in the breeze. They were happy I'd returned, Lilika said. They asked if I remembered Panos, the gentleman who'd come with them the last time. Of course I did. Sadly, they told me, he'd passed away just a few months earlier. The whole town missed him terribly. He had vowed to tend his sheep until the day he died, and that's just how he went—slumped against the wall of his barn up on the hillside, where his heart stopped beating.

"Will you write about my grandmother, all the stories I told you?"

Annula asked. "Will you put these stories in your book?" I explained that that was, in part, why I'd come: to ask her permission to write these things down. At this, she began to cry with happiness.

"Without conversations," Svetlana Boym wrote of her grandmother's recollections of her Soviet childhood, "the memories turn into stones or fairy tales." Annula worried, as many of us do, that her family's stories would vanish when she did. These stories of identity, stories about where and how we belong, are the sorts we clutch tightly, like the keys to fabled, faraway homes.

23.

So stories were tricky creatures, useful for many contradictory ends: they could both commemorate and conjure the past; could separate insider from outsider; could proclaim innocence or guilt; could be a mechanism of theft or of deliverance. Stories could disappear someone into the oblivion of a prison cell or bring someone else back from the dead.

I wanted to write stories that might, by bringing further attention to an issue of social concern, make it possible for something concrete to change, and to enact change on a significant scale. But I wasn't naive; over the years I'd come to see that most journalism had little tangible impact in the end. Still, writing about injustice seemed more useful than doing nothing about it at all, and often positive change was incremental, cumulative. And, bearing in mind that sometimes we can see ourselves with fresher eyes in an image captured from the side rather than one taken head-on, as if in a mirror, I thought that by writing about a place so far from my home I might see my home differently, and help others to do the same.

Frustrated as I was in my efforts to report on the Moria 6, I decided to switch gears for a while and report on pushbacks. On Chios, I met with Antonis Bourmas, a schoolteacher who lived by the sea. His house clung

"You know it's up to you to save these people," he said, filling our tiny glasses. "And I didn't do it." We clinked. It was only midday, but we tipped our heads back as the tsipouro burned its way down our throats.

Back on Lesbos, I received an alert from an activist group: around dawn, thirty-four Eritreans and Somalis between the ages of three and fifty had landed on the southern end of the island. The passengers had contacted Aegean Boat Report, a one-man operation out of northern Norway that documents Aegean crossings and attempts, largely in vain, to make sure that refugees receive protection instead of being covertly expelled. Tommy Olsen, the relentless activist who started Aegean Boat Report in 2017, worked to get the word out about the new arrivals. Meanwhile, the refugees contacted the UN High Commissioner for Refugees hotline.

"The group is still in hiding," Olsen wrote on Facebook that night, "afraid that if authorities [find] them, they will be illegally returned to Turkey." His post was accompanied by photos of people bundled up in an undisclosed inland forest less than a mile from the coast, their faces blurred. "We need UN guarantee that they take us to camp not Turkey," one of the refugees wrote to the United Nations representatives in Greece. But no such guarantee came, and by that evening, still no one had come to their aid.

A man in the group sent Olsen a string of voice memos, his voice hushed over the sound of rustling leaves. "My language no good, I speak Arabic, little English. We are group, thirty-four person, we have four child, please help me, please help us, please help us. We wait here in our place. I'll send you new location." He sent texts, too. "We are 34 people, we have been many hours in the jungle. Children with us. They are crying for hungry and cold please come us soon. Some of us are about to dying for hungry and cold. Please and please help us soon." But no one did.

Not long ago, an arriving boat would be met by dozens of volunteers on the shores of the Aegean—there were sometimes more volunteers than passengers. But today, newcomers are largely left to their own devices when they land. The volunteers are afraid, and they have reason to be. In recent years, along with criminalizing the refugees themselves, the Greek government has been intimidating, arresting, and criminally charging volunteers and NGO workers, as Italy has done to Pia Klemp and the United States to Scott Warren. In 2018, twenty-four humanitarian workers, mostly international volunteers conducting lifesaving rescues in Greek waters, were charged with multiple felonies and misdemeanors carrying penalties of up to twenty-five years in prison. In 2023, the Greek government would charge Olsen himself with "forming or joining for profit and by profession a criminal organization with the purpose of facilitating the entry and stay of third country nationals into Greek territory," for the activities of Aegean Boat Report.

In 2021, the UN Special Rapporteur on Human Rights Defenders held a hearing on the status of humanitarian workers in Greece. "Collectively," she wrote, "the defenders' testimonies painted an extremely concerning picture of the environment for working to see the human rights of all protected and realised in the country." Many of the people who testified spoke of "intimidation, threats and physical attacks" by right-wing groups and even, the police, as well as smear campaigns from within the government. "It was disturbing," observed the Special Rapporteur, "to hear how the fear of arbitrary arrest had deterred some of the participants from carrying out their human rights work and offering humanitarian aid to people at the border of the European Union."

After learning about the group of thirty-four on Lesbos, I drove toward the island's south, past the mountainous region where the group was supposedly hiding. *You know it's up to you to save these people,* Antonis had said. *And I didn't do it.* Don't get arrested, my editor had told me, as had my mother and my husband. I had no intention of getting arrested. But what would be the cost of my inaction? Choosing not to intertwine my story with theirs wouldn't save me from being complicit in whatever became of them.

By the time I was driving south, I knew, the group would have endured three days in the elements with no food or water—if they were still on the island at all. I thought of Wendy Brown's question: "When does the fortress become a penitentiary?" The increasing normalcy of border violence can numb us insiders, making us believe in myths—hidden giants, marauding invaders coming to take what's ours—and in lies: that pushbacks aren't really happening or, perhaps, worse, that they have nothing to do with us, and there's nothing we can do to intervene.

Eventually Olsen sent an update on the Lesbos 34. Their messages had become more desperate. They had moved deeper into the woods, splitting into smaller clusters, then coming together again in their attempts to stay hidden and to survive. In one message he shared, a woman spoke breathlessly into the phone: "Hello, help me, help me, I'm here with a baby, please, please help me."

"The children will die of starvation," a text message read. "And so will we."

A group made their way to one of the island's best-known churches and, at Olsen's urging, took pictures of themselves in front of it. "It would now be extremely difficult to deny their presence on the island, or impossible," Olsen posted to his blog. They found a spot to hide nearby and texted him that a car was approaching. They suspected it was the police. After that, Olsen didn't hear from them again.

The next day, the Turkish Coast Guard announced that they had found a lifeboat carrying twenty-three people—twelve from Eritrea and eleven from Somalia—who said that they'd spent nearly three days in hiding on Lesbos. The people in photos published by the Turkish authorities matched those in the pictures the group had sent Olsen. What had happened to the other eleven people wasn't clear, but what was certain was that the remaining twenty-three had been forcibly removed from Greece, blocked from seeking asylum. Still, the Greek government continued to declare pushbacks were mere fiction.

Thanasis, the interpreter, told me a story his grandfather used to tell him when he was a little boy. When Smyrna was burning, the story went, the Greeks were forced to jump into the water and swim for their lives. British warships were stationed in the harbor, but as the refugees grasped at the gunwales of the boats, soldiers leaned over with swords and chopped off their hands, leaving them to drown. According to some versions, the commanders bid musicians to play their instruments louder in order to blot out the screams.

Factual or not, this story has been passed down through the generations of many families in Greece—those hailing from Asia Minor and otherwise. And it stuck with Thanasis, this image of desperate people swimming—and those situated safely on the boats who, instead of pulling the refugees aboard, severed their outstretched hands. When the contemporary refugee crisis began in 2015, he watched the news with growing concern. Soon he cashed in his savings and moved to

Lesbos to volunteer on the rescue vessels. His grandfather, a communist, had served in the resistance under the Nazi occupation. It was his grandfather's moral life, and that foundational story he'd been told of the refugees in Smyrna, that motivated him to go.

"I was reaching out my hand to pull the people from the water," he told me. He thrust his arm forward as demonstration. "I was reaching out my hand."

As Thanasis, Antonis, and I drank our tsipouro that afternoon in Chios, I asked their thoughts about what advocates were calling the "chilling effect"—the idea that humanitarians are frozen into inaction out of fear of repercussions if they intervene. What if a hundred people, two hundred people, turned up and surrounded the new arrivals, preventing a pushback? Surely the government wouldn't arrest them all, I suggested.

"They would," Thanasis said.

"Maybe," Antonis agreed. "But if we say we believe these things, we must act."

24.

Back in the United States, as I'd been doing for years in the wake of my previous book about unaccompanied minors from El Salvador, I continued to speak about the brutality of contemporary borders to audiences around the country, and people continued to ask me: So what is the answer? Anti-immigrant sentiment was growing the world over, in tandem with the circumstances that spurred migration in the first place. Surely places like the United States and Greece and Germany and Australia can't just take in everyone from around the world, people said, or implied. Where to even begin?

I often pointed to the matter of root causes: people head from their homes to Europe and the United States because something about home has become unlivable. And the things that have made home unlivable are often due, at least in part, to imperial legacies, contemporary corruption, foreign plunder, environmental pillage, and capitalist greed. Until those conditions are sorted, the departures will not cease.

But there were concrete policy changes to consider on the receiving end of migration, too. Doing away with immigration detention, for one. Seeking refuge is legal under international and most domestic laws, and yet doing so is now treated like a crime. This is intentional: if immigrants are locked up as if they are criminals, it will be easier to cement them as such in the imagination of the body politic. Locking them up also affects the outcomes of their immigration cases. In the United

States, an immigrant is far less likely to be able to access legal services from behind bars—only 16 percent do, according to a 2016 study—and yet those armed with an attorney are roughly ten times as likely to win immigration relief as those who are not.

While ending immigration detention is a critical matter of human rights, as I wrote in a 2021 op-ed for *The New York Times*, it would also be a boon to taxpayers. Since the Department of Homeland Security was created in 2002, the federal government has spent an estimated $333 billion on immigration enforcement. In 2018, it spent almost $3.1 billion on detention alone.

There are alternatives to detention that have proven far more humane and also much cheaper. Belgium, for instance, employs a case management model and provides housing, education, and employment services to its newcomers while they are going through the asylum process. The United States piloted a similar if far less robust program, provisionally releasing people from detention while providing family case management services and regular check-ins with US authorities. Before the Trump administration essentially ended the program, 99 percent of the people enrolled in it showed up at their court hearings—meaning they didn't simply go into hiding, as reactionary mythology assumed they would, once they were released from detention. While it costs taxpayers roughly $134 a day to keep someone in a detention center, the alternatives, such as case management and electronic monitoring, cost an average of roughly $4 each day.

So with will, things could be changed. But the more I reported in Europe, the more I understood that another urgent change was in the way the story is told. We needed to revise the story that immigrants are a long-term drain on society, which is simply not backed up by facts.

Destination countries like the United States and Greece treat refugees as a burden to be managed rather than as people—people offering resources and gifts to the place where they arrive. Respecting human rights shouldn't be contingent on whether the humans in question can provide financial benefits, but it's also critical to reject the wildly false narrative that, as Trump put it, "illegal immigration hurts American workers; burdens American taxpayers; undermines public safety; and places enormous strains on local schools, hospitals and communities in general, taking precious resources away from the poorest Americans who need them most."

Even in the George W. Bush administration, a Department of Labor report contended that the notion that undocumented people are a drain on the economy is "the most persistent fallacy about immigration in popular thought." There is no fixed number of jobs in the economy. Jobs are created by the demands and size of the populace. Immigrants fuel our economy. Immigrant households represent a massive tax base, paying $492 billion in total taxes for 2019 alone. Even those without papers pay their share, recorded at $30.6 billion in taxes for that same year. Countering another myth, immigrants also are net contributors to public benefit programs, not drains on them, and help ensure access for everyone with tens of billions of dollars to Social Security and Medicare in 2019. "Without their contributions to the public treasury," writes the American Civil Liberties Union, "the economy would suffer enormous losses." A recent study from the Center for American Progress and the Global Migration Center at the University of California, Davis, showed that if offered a pathway to citizenship, undocumented immigrants would increase the US GDP by $1.7 trillion and create some 500,000 new US jobs.

Another myth undergirding contemporary immigration exclusions (one I've heard within my own Greek American family) is that there simply isn't any more room for newcomers. Yet in the United States and throughout Europe, birth rates are declining; many cities and towns are losing people, neighborhood businesses are shuttering and homes sit empty, schools are closing down. Former industry towns like Buffalo, New York, and Lewiston, Maine, have relied on the US refugee resettlement program to revive them. Rutland, Vermont, a town of roughly sixteen thousand, was losing one hundred residents a year as people died or moved away. In 2016, the mayor begged the State of Vermont to begin resettling refugees there. Two Syrian families were resettled to the city in 2017. A number of Afghans were offered homes there in 2021 when their country fell to the Taliban. The state planned to resettle seventy-five people there in 2023.

In southern Europe, small towns are also emptying. Mayors throughout the region have decided that their only hope is for foreigners to come and repopulate their towns—but by that they mean a certain kind of foreigner, those, above all, with money. Municipalities throughout Greece and Italy have launched one-euro house schemes. They take old buildings that are abandoned or whose owners are no longer able or willing to maintain them and start the bid at one euro apiece, advertising largely to people from the United States and northern Europe. In exchange, buyers agree to renovate the buildings using local labor and to live in their new house for a certain period of time or to make something of it—a business, a community center, some engine of activity and capital that will bring back life to a town turning to ruin.

But some towns in Italy have come to understand that it's not only moneyed foreigners to whom they might profitably open the door, but also the migrants already begging for entry. Sutera, Italy, for instance, launched a resettlement program in 2014 as an effort toward revival. "Every year Sutera lost 300 citizens, due to unemployment," the mayor told *The Guardian*. "The houses emptied, the shops closed and [we] risked becoming a ghost town." Before the refugees began arriving, there were only ten pupils in the local school—so few, it teetered on the brink of shutdown. Today's resettlement program is in fact part of a historic migration continuum; for thousands of years, the town served as a protected mountain refuge for those fleeing conflicts across the Mediterranean. It was never a place of a single people, for there is no such town on earth. "To the townspeople," *The Guardian* wrote, the Sutera refugee program reveals "what Italy's ailing countryside most needs: new life."

Naturally, such resettlement programs have drawn the ire of Italy's far right, who subscribe to the Great Replacement Theory—the notion that, among other things, non-white immigrants are replacing white nationals in "the West" via immigration, and that this is a plan (believed, sometimes, to be orchestrated by "the Jews") intended to eradicate the white race. This theory is a global one—a favorite of Fox News and Newsmax hosts, of Greek and Italian and Norwegian and French white nationalists and far-right political leaders, and of US terrorists like Payton Gendron, who murdered ten people and injured three in a Buffalo supermarket in 2022. "Networks among the nationalist far right are, perhaps paradoxically, increasingly transnational," writes the activist Harsha Walia. The ideology proliferates throughout the internet via memes and chat rooms, bolstered by existing racism as well as political rhetoric—the insistence that end times are coming thanks to brown people crossing the borders and that, for any personal misfortune, there is someone to blame.

The reactionary movement seems to have been bolstered by the boom in genetic services like 23andMe. White nationalist forums like Stormfront reveal an obsession with such tests. Chat room members frequently use the results to claim racial superiority and to perpetuate the made-up myth of whiteness.

I know very well that the hunger for a home, and a homeland, is a human one. But these genetic services have carved a slippery slope toward genetic determinism—which "reduces the self to a molecular entity, equating human beings, in all their social, historical, and moral complexity, with their genes," explain Dorothy Nelkin and Susan Lindee in their book *The DNA Mystique: The Gene as a Cultural Icon.* We humans are infinitely much more the same than we are different. What genetic research has, in fact, made abundantly clear is that race is a myth—since all humans trace back to the first *Homo sapiens* in Africa, and any assertion of racial or national purity is, in both genetic and historic terms, a lie—an attempt at identity apartheid, a galvanizing force for barricade.

25.

In the course of my reporting, I learned about a man who seemed as if he might have some of the answers I was seeking about how to make meaningful change within a vast system of oppression: Dimitris Choulis, a lawyer on Samos. That island, too, had received thousands of refugees over the years, and many were now being spirited away via the pushback regime. On Samos, as on Lesbos and other islands, human rights defenders had learned to stay away from the arrival sites so as not to risk arrest or retribution from the authorities. But not Choulis. He still managed to meet the new arrivals regularly, I'd heard, intercepting them before they were found by authorities without being arrested or charged himself.

I arranged to meet Choulis on an overcast day in the main square of Vathy, across from the harbor where the Coast Guard boats docked. I spotted him from my seat in the café. A hoodie was cinched tightly against his face and jammed in his pocket was an oversize umbrella. He was on his way to court, he told me, but he had a few minutes to chat.

I got right down to it: how did he do the work he did without getting arrested?

"Everyone asks me this," he said. He signaled to the waiter and ordered a tea. "What people have to understand is that Greece is still a country, with laws, and I am merely using those laws and making sure they are followed." New arrivals to Samos contacted him all the time, having gotten his number through the Facebook and WhatsApp grapevine. As soon as he heard from them and verified their location within Greek territory, he simply alerted the local authorities and the Ministry of Migration in Athens, letting them know that a new group had arrived and that, as a human rights attorney, he was on his way to meet them.

He made his work sound simple—and, in his eyes, it apparently was. But if it was indeed so simple, why weren't other human rights attorneys on other islands using these same strategies? He shrugged—he couldn't speak for them, he said. This stuck with me. One is responsible, above all, for one's own actions and inactions—the rest is between you and your God, or between you and yourself.

If Choulis's protocol was simple, things weren't exactly easy for him. He had been born and raised on Samos, but even as a local he was regularly threatened by other islanders who felt his advocacy on behalf of migrants only drew more people to the island. His family also received threats: menacing phone calls, warnings of bodily harm. And he'd managed to attract the ire of Athens, too. A few weeks before I met him in the square, a delegation of European Parliament members had visited Samos to learn more about the refugee situation in the Aegean, and about pushbacks in particular. During their stay, a boat landed and, as had become standard, the refugees who had been aboard fled into hiding in the woods and contacted Choulis. He invited one of the parliamentarians to accompany him when he met with the refugees. The MP was horrified at the group's situation, and in fear of what would befall them at the hands of authorities, decided to tweet about it. Greece's minister of migration took to Twitter to slam Choulis and to announce that he would be investigated for his work with refugees, even though the minister of migration is not responsible for criminal investigations.

"Let them try me," Choulis answered coolly when I asked him about it. "I've done nothing wrong." And as for the local harassment, he wasn't worried about it, either.

"Poverty didn't make me leave. Breaking up with my girlfriend and seeing her in the square with her new boyfriend didn't make me leave," he told me. "So how can these threats make me leave the island?" Samos was where he was from.

His tea arrived, and I watched as he tore open six packets of sugar and stirred them into his mug. "Are you going to use this?" he asked, pointing to my small pot of honey. I was not. This, too, he stirred into his tea.

Choulis struck me as a man in constant motion, not unlike a hummingbird—a man whose life was, it seemed, made entirely of action.

In addition to criminalizing the work of human rights defenders like Choulis and the twenty-four humanitarian workers, Greece was criminalizing journalists. In November 2020, a Canadian journalist documenting pushbacks was arrested on a charge of smuggling, his car and equipment confiscated. He was deported and is prohibited from visiting Greece again. In 2021, several Greek journalists learned that they were being spied on by the center-right New Democracy government for their reporting on migration and government corruption. They were being followed, their phones tapped, their texts monitored. One of the journalists being surveilled in Greece had reported on the horrific conditions of Moria and on possible corruption within camp management, including allegations that officials had inflated the number of refugees living in Moria so they could collect more funds from the EU.

The situation for Greek journalists continued to deteriorate. In 2022, authorities arrested two photojournalists while they were on the job. Meanwhile, a journalist writing about organized crime was executed in broad daylight, and two other journalists found makeshift bombs outside their homes—crimes the government appeared to do little to investigate. Between 2021 and 2022, Greece plummeted from 70 to 108 in its ranking in the Reporters Without Borders World Press Freedom Index—the lowest of any country in Europe.

Already the United States was adopting a similar playbook under President Trump, creating a database of activists, immigration attorneys, and journalists working at the US–Mexico border in order to monitor their activities and even, in some cases, to restrict their ability to move back and forth across the border. Such tactics of surveillance, intimidation, and criminalization of human rights workers and the press—wherever they occur—are clear in their intent: to curb not only lifesaving assistance to refugees, but also the coverage of the injustices waged against them.

In late 2021, the Greek government instituted a new law against so-called fake news. It was astoundingly broad, threatening prison time to "anyone who publicly or via the internet spreads or disseminates in any way false news that is capable of causing concern or fear to the public or shattering public confidence in the national economy, the country's defense capacity or public health." The trouble with combating fake news, as those of us living in the United States know all too well, is that it puts the very definition of reality up for debate. The arbiter of such a sweeping law is whoever happens to be in power. No matter how much I struggled with the constraints of journalism, I knew that journalism could in fact thwart not only abuses of power but also these very perversions of reality.

. . .

In late 2021, the news outlet Lighthouse Reports published an extensive and damning article on mass expulsions throughout Europe, with footage of what were undeniably pushbacks taking place in Greece. Because the Coast Guard routinely confiscates or destroys the phones of those it intercepts, such footage is rare. But even before this report, there was no longer any plausible denial that pushbacks were taking place. At a November press conference after the report was released, a Dutch journalist named Ingeborg Beugel said as much to the Greek prime minister.

"Prime Minister Mitsotakis, when, at last, will you stop lying? Lying about pushbacks, lying about what is happening with the refugees in Greece?" she asked. "There has been overwhelming evidence, and you keep denying and lying. . . . Why are you not honest? . . . Why don't you say, 'Brussels left us alone. We waited for six years, nobody did anything, we need to relocate, they don't do it . . . and yes, I do cruel, barbarian pushbacks'?"

Mitsotakis could barely mask his scorn. "I understand that in the Netherlands you have a culture of asking direct questions to politicians, which I very much respect," he said. "What I will not accept is that in this office you will insult me or the Greek people with accusations and expressions that are not supported by material facts." No matter that material facts about pushbacks abounded, and he knew it.

Earlier that fall, I had put the question of pushbacks to Governor Moutzouris on Lesbos. "Because you are recording," he told me with a smile, pointing to my iPhone on the table, "I will say that there are no pushbacks."

This is the plain doublespeak of autocracy—another thing we are no strangers to in the United States. Take, for instance, the attorney for the Department of Justice arguing in a public courtroom in 2019 that providing soap and toothbrushes to detained immigrant children wasn't necessary as part of the government's obligations to provide them "safe and sanitary" conditions.

Sometimes the way to counter such maneuvers and denials of reality is to mimic them. Dimitris Choulis told me about a time he'd arrived too late to meet a group of refugees. The police had already found the group and detained them inside their vans.

"Here," Choulis told the officers, handing them bags of provisions. "Give them this water and this food."

"We don't know what you're talking about," he recalls the police saying. They insisted there weren't any refugees.

"Okay," said Choulis. "If you find them, give them the water. And if you don't find them, please also give them the water."

There was the question of how to communicate within authoritarian regimes, but especially for those without the protections of a particular citizenship, race, or class, there was also the matter of how to survive them. As ever, looking backward offered clues.

When the Nazis invaded Greece, they ascended the Acropolis hill and hoisted a hulking swastika flag in front of the Parthenon for all to see. "Unlike other conquered countries," writes historian Roderick Beaton, "Greece seems to have been viewed by the Nazis as booty to be plundered and picked clean, rather than as a going concern to be nurtured and maintained in their own interest." The occupiers stole ancient artifacts, destroyed entire villages, and executed suspected dissenters at will. Eighty thousand Greek Jews were sent to the concentration camps, mostly to Auschwitz. The Nazis were thorough in their genocide there: by the time the war ended, hardly any Jews were left in Greece.

The Nazis also plundered the nation's food supply to feed their armies throughout Europe. By the time the war ended, writes Beaton, an additional estimated 250,000 Greeks had died of starvation.

"When the Germans came, they took all our food away from us," a Cretan grandmother recalled to her daughter-in-law about the war. The Germans executed her father by firing squad, forcing her and her mother to watch, and killed her brother, too. "From one day to the next, we were thrown into the depths of poverty." The Nazis killed at will, and took the Greeks' crops and their animals; there was no meat left, no bread, hardly anything they could eat. "We could go and pick the fruits off our trees in our orchards, but if the Germans saw us on the road carrying them back to our house, they'd confiscate them."

Foraging in the wild proved to be a loophole, for the items they carried back from the hillsides or coasts—snails, amaranth, nettles, dandelion—didn't seem to strike the Germans as food. Horta was the name for a class of plants that grew wild throughout Greece. Stewed and boiled, horta has been a staple of the Greek diet since the post-Neolithic period, with families passing down the lore of where to find it in the hillsides to this day.

To the Nazis, this horta was mere weeds, nothing—but rich with minerals, it helped sustain many Greeks under the occupation, allowing them to keep on living. Like Choulis's verbal trickery, the horta story suggests that, sometimes, authoritarianism can be navigated by channeling one's skills, inherited knowledge, and secrets into a strategy of cunning.

. . .

Shortly after meeting Choulis, I spoke to a man from Senegal I'll call Pascal, who had crossed to Lesbos a few months earlier.

On his first try, he had been intercepted by the authorities at sea—the Greek Coast Guard, he thought. A speedboat had turned doughnuts around them, flooding their boat with water; then the crew, who were masked, beat back with batons anyone who tried to board their vessel and pierced the pontoons of the refugees' boat, after which they towed it back out to sea and left them there. The refugees began sinking.

"This has happened to me before," one of Pascal's fellow passengers said as their boat deflated—meaning he'd been pushed back on a prior attempt. "But this time they really seem like they are trying to kill us."

Minutes before their boat was fully submerged, which would have drowned them all, the Turkish Coast Guard arrived and plucked them from the sea.

Months later, Pascal boarded another boat. He made it all the way to Lesbos this time. His group knew that the next step was to stay hidden until they could make their way to camp, in order to register before being found by the police. The camp was over a hundred kilometers away. The group splintered into smaller pods to avoid detection; soon it was just Pascal and another man making their way south together. "We were two Black people," he told me, "on an island full of whites."

Pascal knew that more than anything, though, it was their clothes that made them stand out. They were dirty and wet after the crossing, so it was clear to anyone they happened upon that they were new arrivals rather than registered refugees who had been on the island for some time. Yes, they were racing the clock to get to the camp, but the most pressing matter, Pascal decided, was to acquire new outfits. They arrived at a small town in the middle of the island, where they passed a store run by a man of Asian descent. This was another immigrant, Pascal thought—someone who was less likely than a Greek to rat them out. They hurried into the store and, with the little money they had, each bought a fresh pair of pants and a shirt; they discarded their dirty clothes in the garbage. They walked back into the town square, heads held high with feigned confidence, and used their phones to find a bus to take them to the camp. When the bus pulled up, they walked right on board, as if it were something they did every day. And when they reached the camp, they stepped off and presented themselves for registration. They were safe for now—they could apply for asylum, and no one could turn them back until they saw that process through. Pascal had outsmarted the system built to keep him from existing on that island at all.

I stayed on the lookout for such stories of cunning, wanting to make space for the agency and ingenuity of advocates, yes, and also for that of migrants themselves, who are so often cast in the narratives of others as mere victims. And I wanted to learn from such stories whether, read side by side, they could provide a road map for survival, action, and solidarity in increasingly hostile territory.

In the fall of 2022, Greek Twitter lit up with the story of a man named Michalis Protopsaltis. He was a crane operator on the island of Kythera who spent long days outside, helping to construct homes all over the island. One night, he was settling in at home after a long, tiring day of work. He had pulled off his shoes and poured himself a glass of wine when he noticed out his window that the sea was rough, the waves hurling themselves against the island's cliffs. "God save those who are at its mercy tonight," he said to himself as he lay down and switched on the TV.

Soon, as if he'd known they'd be coming, he heard voices shouting down at the shore. Dozens of them, maybe more—but he had no idea what they were saying, for they weren't speaking Greek. The rocks near his home were "high and sharp," as he put it, and anyone caught there was in trouble. He had to help whoever it was, he knew. So he put his shoes back on and stepped into his crane, then drove toward the voices. There they were in the water below: eighty people flailing in the chop, screaming for help.

He hung the sandbag and dipped the crane into the ocean. The sandbag was big enough for two people to hold on to it at a time while he lifted them back up to land. "The waves were wild, deadly," he recalled. He lowered the crane and lifted, lowered and lifted, hoisting the travelers from the water two by two. He'd never run the crane that hard before. "Even though they say that souls are like feathers, they are heavier than iron," he would later comment. He worked until he'd pulled eighty people up to shore, until no one was left shouting in the frothing sea below.

Once he'd done all he could, he leaned against his truck, "the engine still running like a praying mother," he said. "I cried. The sea was screaming below."

After a humanitarian group had arrived to take the survivors to safety, he returned home, drank his glass of wine in a single gulp, and lay down again. He'd later learn that ten people lost their lives in that shipwreck. He'd suspected that night that he hadn't been able to reach them all. He had always believed that the materials he used to build houses had souls of sorts—the concrete, the iron, all of it came from somewhere on the earth. Some of the homes he worked on were built strictly legally with all the right permits and permissions, some not. And here were all these people who had just landed on his island and whom he had lifted with his crane. What did it matter whether they had papers? He crossed himself and slipped into an easy sleep. "I felt like I had no weight, like a feather," he said. "I didn't watch the news that night."

The news wasn't getting any better, the injustices seemed to deepen every day, but the more such stories I heard, the more I understood that focusing on scale could be a psychic trap—one that could limit the imagination and hamstring the effort to act at all. Protopsaltis was just a man with a machine; his act was remarkable by the very virtue of being singular, but that didn't mean it didn't matter—that it didn't make a significant difference. Such acts—outsmarting the border authorities, interrupting a single pushback, leaving water for migrants in the desert, even writing an article that exposed some wrongdoing—could be interruptions of injustice even when they could not eradicate it. They had value—more value than I, in my frustration and impatience, had been affording them.

I came across a story about the surrealist poet Robert Desnos that buoyed this line of thinking. In an essay titled "To Love the Marigold: Hope & Imagination," Susan Griffin recounts that Desnos, as a Jew working in the French Resistance, was imprisoned in several concentration camps during the war, including Auschwitz. One day, the guards loaded him and other prisoners onto a truck without explanation. The group knew that they were being taken to the gas chambers. This was the end.

Except that, as a surrealist, Desnos had dabbled in the occult and in palm reading. So when the group arrived at its destination and was about to be unloaded, he leaped up, grabbed the hands of one of his companions, and began to read the man's future. "Oh," he said, according to a story Griffin once heard, "I see you have a very long lifeline." Desnos was exuberant. "First one man, then another, offers up his hand," writes Griffin, "and the prediction is for longevity, more children, abundant joy."

I can picture him there, defying death with these stories of the future. *You too will live a long life!* I imagine him shouting while staring into palm after palm. *You will take your children to the seaside next summer, and your son's face will freckle like a collection of stars! You will become a great singer on Europe's most gilded of stages! You will have a daughter, and another daughter, and another, and they will each have three daughters.* And on and on and on.

So stunned were the condemned prisoners, the story goes, that they began to smile. Another person offered up his hand to Desnos, and then another, to receive their futures like a final meal, or last rites. His fortune-telling seemed to spook the guards with the notion that these walking dead could have some fate in store other than the gas chamber. "If they told themselves these deaths were inevitable," Griffin reflects, "this no longer seems inarguable. They are in any case so disoriented by this sudden change of mood among those they are about to kill that they are unable to go through with the executions." The prisoners were taken back to the barracks; some of them lived to see the end of the war, and their own liberation, thanks to Desnos's act.

It's unclear whether this story of exuberant, cunning defiance is entirely true or somewhat apocryphal, but I don't mind either way. "Can the imagination save us?" Griffin asks. "Robert Desnos was famous for his belief in the imagination. He believed it could transform society." Of course he didn't stop the Holocaust, didn't close his camp, didn't even likely keep many of the people he saved that day from ultimately dying at the Nazis' hands. What he did was imagine a reality different from the gas chambers, and then he enacted that story in the world, determined, even for a moment, to make it come true.

26.

If I were to write ethically and well about Moria, and about the vast machinery of global immigration enforcement, I would have to portray these small acts of resistance alongside urgent calls for sweeping change. It also seemed vital to zoom out and consider migration in the broader sense: how it mapped with ecology and geological time.

People have always had to move upon this earth—in search of food, in search of safety, in search of more favorable conditions to build a home. Before there were countries with borders there were merely regions, and before that just the earth itself—travel far enough back in time and there weren't even continents separated by water, only one big mass of land.

I began to research the way forests, like humans, moved over millennia. If you look at a sped-up map, you'll see that forests have been racing up and down the planet as ice ages have come and gone. As I was reporting about forced migration in Greece, I got an assignment to write about something called assisted species migration—the practice that, given that forests naturally move in the direction better suited for their growth yet cannot move fast enough to outrun climate change, "moves" forests in advance of their demise. If we want these trees to survive, in other words, they need our assistance—we must help them move.

I soon became entranced with forests and their inner workings. A forest was a striking metaphor. Far more than just a collection of trees, forests are a complex civilization, functioning not unlike human cities: trees talk to one another and organize and defend themselves and create offspring as they bid farewell to their dead. Within a forest, trees live in interdependent networks, like families, where, with the help of symbiotic fungi, they care for their sick, feed one another, and share resources with those in need. Trees of the same species—and sometimes even those across species—tend to respect one another's personal space, shifting their growth patterns so that everyone gets enough sunlight. All the same, trees are adept community organizers who know how to band together to crowd out competitors and guard against other threats. When a pest comes, trees can issue warnings to their community members so that together they can launch their defenses. Trees can also register pain; they may even scream in agony when hurt, at decibels inaudible to the human ear. Scientists have found that their root networks, which work in tandem with the underworld organisms of fungal mycelia, seem to hold intergenerational knowledge, like a collective brain. With certain scientific devices, you can hear the fortified water pumping up from the roots into the tree's core, like an arboreal pulse.

Read enough about the magical science of trees and you might begin to believe that if humans behaved like a healthy forest, we'd be far better off.

But writing about the natural world, even as metaphor, was a portal not only to hope but to more sorrow. As I researched, I traversed my home state, moving through its parched landscapes and its staggering burn zones where everything was charred black, tree carcasses now spearing the skyline, destroyed buildings like upright cadavers. When I went to Greece I saw much of the same: scorched olive groves in Andros, the bleak remnants of a devastating fire on the island of Evia. Time and time again, as when I researched migration, my spirit was brought to its knees.

I traveled to Oregon to meet with scientists who had planted experimental groves of trees to see which would best survive when moved to a new landscape, so they could map out the forests of the future. I visited Joshua Tree, one of my most cherished places on earth. I drove through the park south to north, moving through a low, flat valley where Joshua trees and cholla clustered in mighty stands. Though the Joshua trees there in the valley looked healthy enough, the scientists I spoke to told me otherwise. Look closely, they told me, and you'll see there are no young sprouting among the elders. This was a last generation, not unlike those in the emptied towns of southern Europe, living out their final days as the last of their kind to call that spot home.

From the valley I moved to the highlands, where I saw, in effect, trees that were "running" uphill to cooler, wetter land on an intergenerational march against their own disappearance. These highland trees were lovely from all angles, like benevolent apparitions from some absurdist underworld. But the best view was from above: across the valley floor the Joshua trees were thriving, surrounded by their young, with room still to move upward—for now.

Last of all, I traveled to a bristlecone pine forest at twelve thousand feet in eastern California. There some of the world's oldest trees—the eldest is nearly five thousand years old—stand sentinel over Nevada's Great Basin. As protection against the harshness of their high desert landscape, the bristlecones develop a thick, impervious bark that protects them from pests and fire. The harshness of their environment, in other words, is what grants them longevity. But for them, I learned, this was the last leg, because beyond their hilltop home is only sky.

In all these places I visited, I was coming to appreciate the anatomy of survival, and how entwined the ability to move is with the perpetuation of life on earth.

27.

After the trial, Ali's attorneys immediately filed an appeal, but it would be nearly a year before they were given a date for the new trial.

As the Moria 6 sat in Avlona prison back on the mainland, arrivals on Lesbos slowed overall as a result of pushbacks, and people remained in Mavrovouni, the new Black Mountain camp, just outside town. Most people referred to the camp as "New Moria," for, in the big picture, not all that much had changed when it came to the refugees' sense of well-being or future prospects. While security in the new camp was better, and it was far less crowded, people's movements in and out were now severely restricted. The camp flooded in rain and high winds, and at least a dozen accidental fires, sparked by cookstoves or illicit heaters, blazed within the first year of its opening, as they used to in Moria.

Meanwhile, the Ministry of Migration was working to make good on its promise to build new camps on the Aegean Islands that more closely resembled the US detention model: closed, prisonlike facilities vastly more restrictive than Mavrovouni even, and far from support resources and human rights monitors in the urban centers. In September 2021, almost exactly a year after the Moria fire, the first such camp opened in Samos. With its upgraded facilities and state-of-the-art surveillance systems, it cost 43 million euros to build.

In protest, Governor Moutzouris refused to go to the opening. "We don't want these camps built on our islands," he told me—not the sprawling catastrophes like Moria, not the "controlled access centers" like the new one on Samos. Such camps, he and other conservatives like him felt, ensured the continued presence of refugees on his islands. But the Samos facility was widely decried also by humanitarian workers, who saw it as one step closer to a prison.

"There is no doubt that this new centre will only further dehumanise and marginalise people seeking protection in the European Union," wrote Médecins Sans Frontières days before the camp was set to open. "For the people undergoing these violent migration policies, the opening of this new centre marks an 'end': an end to the meaning of life, to their patience, to any rudimentary freedom they had." Like the locking away of the Moria 6 and the pushback regime, these camps were yet another disappearing act in an elaborate disappearance parade.

When people in Greece discussed the new camps and decried the closed conditions, I noticed a faint voice in my head: *Well, at least they can leave sometimes.* In the United States, after all, immigration detention wasn't just *like* prison, it was actual prison. This faint voice disturbed me deeply for it revealed to me that, in the course of reporting on the terrors of closed immigration facilities, I had also been infected by the impulse to normalize them. This is how the redefinition of reality functions—it can work us over, reconfiguring what we notice and how we see the world, how we tell its stories.

A week after the anniversary of the Moria fire, five hundred refugees on the island of Samos were to be moved, largely against their will, to the hulking, fenced-in camp twenty miles out of town, where bright lights would be kept on all through the night. When later reporting from the town of Vathy, I'd be able to see the lights painting the sky from miles away. The night before the residents were moved, another massive fire erupted in back of the old camp, destroying several shipping containers but injuring no one.

Soon after opening the Samos facility, the Ministry of Migration opened another such camp on the island of Kos, and then another on Leros. Opponents on Lesbos were able to stave off the construction of their own closed camp for a few months, but in January 2022, the ministry finally broke ground in Vastria, about an hour north of the capital city.

The protesters came in droves. At first the actions were peaceful, but matters quickly escalated. On February 7, an estimated three to four hundred people arrived at the construction site and barreled past police, who, the paper noted, did nothing to stop the mob. Protesters set fire to the generator supplying power to the construction site and knocked down the porta-potties, then ignited the bulldozers and excavators. As night fell, the machines burned and glowered like automated agents of the apocalypse.

By the following morning, six people had been arrested by the police and charged with nearly a dozen crimes, including inciting violence against employees, disturbing the peace, arson, unlawful violence, and sedition. The symmetry with the Moria fire was stunning: another six arrested, for setting aflame yet another camp hardly anyone wanted.

28.

On each trip to Greece, exhausted from travel and reporting, I would spend my final night on Andros, the island of my ancestors, where I'd float in the sea and drink from the enchanted springs. Though I looked for them, I didn't again encounter the hypericum blooming in the steep valley or the possessed donkey that had set its teeth on Ben.

On the mainland, I'd met with Lefteris Arapakis, a fifth-generation fisherman working in Piraeus, the country's largest port. When Lefteris was a boy, he'd join his father at the docks or voyage out to sea with his crew, helping to release the nets and pull them back up. Sometimes the nets snagged on something on the ocean floor and had to be cut loose. These ghost nets, made of plastic, would spend eternity clogging the waterways, continuing to fish.

And up on deck, the crews were catching plastic along with fish. Sometimes, Lefteris told me, it made up half a boat's haul. Once, he and a friend dragged up a Coke can from the 1980s—a can that had spent longer in the ocean than Lefteris had spent alive. The captain snatched it from his hand and threw it back into the sea.

Lefteris began to contemplate the travesty of the ocean, all the devastation hidden beneath the surface. He felt compelled to act, but how? He came up with a plan to launch a recycling program, paying fishermen to haul the trash back to shore, where it would be collected and recycled—into socks, into irrigation pipes, into bottles to hold water and soda. His father thought he was out of his mind. "Don't embarrass me," he said. But so far the plan had worked—Lefteris's team had recovered tens of thousands of pounds of garbage from the sea. This was his own tale of cunning, his own survival story.

Because migration is everywhere in Greece, it is central to the Piraeus story, too. Many of the port's fishermen are Egyptian migrant laborers who spend half the year on work visas trawling the Greek seas. As a result, the port became a hot zone of Golden Dawn activity. The neo-Nazis would patrol the harbor with knives and bats, beating up anyone who didn't look Greek or who spoke with an accent, stealing the cash they'd made from their time at sea.

But even Greeks working the Piraeus ports often hailed from elsewhere, Lefteris explained to me. Many of the fishermen, including his grandfather, were descended from the Asia Minor Greeks from what is now Türkiye. It was their fishing boats that had allowed them to make it to Greece alive, to start over.

Lefteris's grandmother, however, was from Andros—just like my great-grandmother. We joked about being cousins. She lived on the mainland now, but spoke often of her old village, whose name Lefteris couldn't recall. It was now just ruins—a few tumbledown houses, nothing more. Because she was losing her memory, he told me, she lived "very far back in the past." It was sad, he said, to watch her mind go, but also somewhat beautiful. Difficult things, like the state of her beloved village, were washed from her mind. She got to keep her story of the past just so.

Since Ben and I had missed it the first time, I was determined to finally visit my great-grandmother's village on Andros, Korthio—the place the immigration records proclaimed she'd been born. I decided to drive through the town one afternoon, taking the long way to catch my ferry back to the mainland.

At the bay of Korthio lay a little beach town, but as I understood it my great-grandmother (and her mother and father) had been born in the smaller town up the hill from the sea. I followed signs in that direction. There seemed to be plenty of service, but all the same, my phone's map went haywire and quickly became useless again, requiring me to be fully in the landscape rather than in its digitized double. I wound past oleander and olive groves, a tiny school, the walls of so many of the buildings now ruins, as if the landscape were taking back its stone. I didn't see a soul. I pulled over at a little chapel that looked out over the valley below. Years before, Pavlos had explained that these roadside churches were built all over this island so that seafaring families could light candles, beseeching God to protect their loved ones out at sea. I wanted to light one, but the door was locked. Oh, well. There weren't enough candles on this island, perhaps on this planet, to secure all the safe passage needed across its lands and seas.

I tried to make my way back to the main road, but my map continued to loop me in panicked circles, so I turned it off; instinct, in spite of the easy waypoint of the sea below, didn't help me much, either. I tried to picture my great-grandmother here as a little girl, but still all I could conjure was the image of her as an old lady, always an immigrant in my mind, never truly belonging where she was. And me? I had a home I was now anxious to get back to—so far away from where all my ancestors had started. Somehow, no matter which way I turned, I kept looping back on the same roads, as if bewitched. I watched this story take shape in my mind even as I was living it: how, when I'd finally made it to Evanthia's birthplace, there wasn't much to see, but the place didn't seem to want to let me go.

Stories help us stave off the sense of ruin—the knowledge that the past is going or is already long gone. I thought of my dad's tale of the fabled chest, the bequeathed land just south of Andros that, if it hadn't been for migration and the slippage of time, might still be ours.

My great-grandmother had left this town of Korthio, on Andros island, for the mainland, and then left Greece altogether, dreaming us all into being in a new country. But as is the case with many descendants of immigrants, my father's mythology looked backward, imagining into existence a past that didn't make us richer, but that made us more deeply belong. And because the past recedes so swiftly and deeply in stories of immigration, we didn't know many of the details of the family's life on Andros—so who's to say what might have been? On this island we could have been goat herders, local nobility, intellectuals, shipping tycoons. We could have been radicals, aristocrats, berry hawkers, bondsmen to the wind. Time insists on moving forward—when stripped of myth and magic, "home" is merely the place you now live. We could have been so many things in that gilded past we've incarnated with our longing. Here at home, instead, we're just us.

29.

When I'd traveled to Thessaloniki en route to the Evros borderline, I'd been stunned to find a small exhibition on the life and work of Svetlana Boym, the theorist whose work had served as a lodestar for me over the years I had been thinking about human beings and their relationship to place, to movement, and to memory.

When Boym was nineteen, she fled Leningrad, renouncing her Soviet citizenship with hopes of resettling in the United States. On the way, she was interned for several months in an austere Vienna transit camp for Soviet refugees—a place, she'd later write, that "resembled a provincial military hospital or a monastery."

"We never saw the Vienna that we dreamed about," she recalled, "the city of Mozart and Freud. We remained extraterritorial. Like the Freudian unconscious, our transit camp had no outside; it was a place out of place and a time out of time." This made me think of Ali, and how he'd dreamed of encountering Athens as a voyager but met the city only as a prisoner.

Eventually, after months in this non-Vienna, Boym made her way to Boston and moved on with her life in "the West." The camp receded from memory. She hadn't taken any pictures of the place and held only a few memories of its particulars—it had been, after all, merely a tunnel between one life and another. "I happily forgot my forgetting," as she put it. "My emigration from Leningrad to Boston had a few detours, gaps, and loose ends. But the point was not to travel on memory lane but to move on, to begin again. Why remember the unmemorable?"

Years later, though, she would return to Vienna for a conference. By then, she'd become an academic and a photographer, drawn to taking pictures of "transits, warzones, afterimages of something we see and forget." She'd often photograph the smallest details, like rubbled concrete or flowers piercing the cracks. While in Vienna, she decided to locate the old transit camp and take its picture, too. But the camp proved hard to find. She wasn't quite sure where it had been, since she'd only been a kid, stuck inside, with no reference to the outside world, and there was no address for this "extraterritorial refuge for extralegal immigrants" in any official records or maps she could get her hands on. The camp, she was coming to understand, had always been an "invisible city."

Since the archives failed her, Boym took her search online, scouring the outskirts of Vienna via Google Earth. She also began interviewing others who had transited through the same camp, asking them to add their memories to a map of the place she'd sketched out on a paper napkin. Everyone seemed to have different recollections of the place, though—both how it had looked and how it had felt, what it had meant to them to be encircled by its walls.

She was determined to find it once and for all, but many of her friends who'd also transited through the camp couldn't see why. "Why revisit the camp now?" Boym wrote. "We were very tough then because we knew how to forget; if we start remembering now we could risk our immigrant resilience. Obsession with the past might shortchange our future."

Through several strokes of luck, Boym eventually figured out where the camp had been—on Dreherstrasse, in an area on the outskirts of Vienna called Simmering. She took her camera with her, and a Greek artist named Maria Zervos tagged along to record her return.

It was Zervos's film that was being exhibited in Thessaloniki the summer I visited. In the museum, I entered a dark, domed room where three rectangular boxes of light projected on a blank wall. The center box displayed footage of Boym walking around the old camp, now just an empty dirt yard rimmed with stone walls and the remnants of machinery. In this film she holds her camera; plants grow among the stones. The outer two frames of the exhibition displayed a slideshow of the photographs Boym was taking with that very camera as she walked around the ruins: a shopping cart filled with pine cones, piles of refuse, a lone poppy against a decaying stone wall. The walls of the camp, she wrote, had "stood both for liberation and for confinement, for memory and for forgetting; they became a canvas for our improbable hopes."

It wasn't until Boym returned to Boston and looked at the pictures she'd taken at the old camp that she realized how closely they resembled those she'd been taking her whole life, all around the world: crumbling walls, barbed wire, small, determined shoots of plant life piercing the remains. "I didn't know until then," she wrote, "that I had been a subject of my photographs and not just a photographer." It was as if she'd been trying to capture the Vienna camp all along—the point of departure that would lead to the rest of her life.

In the final frames of Zervos's film, Boym stands in the middle of the abandoned former camp, encircled by walls. She draws the camera to her face, then leans forward to photograph a wide, shallow puddle. By now, the sun is lowering behind her and casts a long evening shadow across the water. Slowly, slowly, Zervos's camera moves in toward Boym and the puddle until the sun catches Zervos's shadow, too. Like this, these human outlines—observer and subject, both archivists of memory and chroniclers of this invisible city—meet, and nearly touch. Then the film goes black.

30.

Ali waited and waited. As his appeal approached, we stayed in touch, and he continued to share his story with me. I also began speaking with Hassan, another of the Moria 6, who would call me some evenings to ask me how I was. "People don't believe us," he said. "It's good you are writing something." It was terrible to be disbelieved, but his version of the story, he insisted, was true.

I stayed in touch with Sedique and Fatimah, too, the young women I'd met at their picnic in the Moria ruins. In late summer of 2021, they'd started taking art classes with an organization called Wave of Hope in downtown Mytilene and volunteering in its sun-filled gallery space. This meant that they had special permission to leave the camp every day except Sunday; instead of waiting around their tents in Mavrovouni, they could spend their days in town painting, hanging portraits on the wall, greeting visitors, arguing about which hairdo best suited their favorite K-pop star in his Instagram posts.

Sedique was worried about her fifteen-year-old brother, though, who didn't have such an escape hatch from camp. He had been depressed since the fire, feeling stuck in his family's circumstances on Lesbos and worried that they would be deported to Türkiye. He spent most of his days lying in their tent, looking at his phone or sleeping. In the preceding months, the Taliban had been regaining control of Afghanistan, and this news hadn't helped. The family worried about their loved ones back home and about the fate of their country.

Then the Taliban took Kabul. Sedique started to have trouble sleeping. Mehdi's mother, her future mother-in-law, stayed hidden inside her Kabul apartment for weeks. When they needed food, Mehdi's younger brother would steal outside to fetch provisions, which put the whole family on edge for fear of what could happen to him. "They are just kidnapping and killing people," Sedique reported.

The Taliban takeover had led to an unsettling psychic state for many refugees on Lesbos. While people were panic-stricken by what was happening back home, events in Afghanistan made it more likely that those who'd made it this far would actually receive asylum in Greece. It messed with your mind, that such a horrible turn of events could also be a stroke of luck.

The Greek authorities were keeping a keen eye on the situation in Afghanistan, too, knowing it would only send more refugees their way. As the Taliban moved toward Kabul, the Greek government had scrambled to finish fencing along the Turkish border and ramp up its sea patrols.

"We cannot wait, passively, for the possible impact," the Greek minister of civil protection announced within hours of Kabul falling. He was talking about the impact of the Taliban not on Afghanistan but on Greece. "Our borders will remain safe and inviolable," he declared. Reports of pushbacks soared.

The Moria 6 learned the news from home only in drips and drabs. They were terrified for their families. Ali's brother had worked for the Americans, after all. Hassan learned his brother had been imprisoned by the Taliban for a tattoo on his arm—it was nothing political, just a tattoo. His mother was distraught; one son in prison at home, one son in prison many countries away. Like Ali, Hassan knew what was happening with his family, but he could do nothing to help them. The shadow of war and the Taliban were what had made them all leave in the first place, and now the Taliban were back. Though most of the Moria 6 were in touch with their families in Afghanistan, the contact was infrequent. And in truth, most of the young men had lied about or downplayed what had happened to them in Greece in order to protect their families, trying not to lay a heavier burden on their crumbling worlds.

"I'm going to die because of what's happened to you," Ali's mother wailed when she found out her son was locked up. Anytime he'd been able to speak to her, he told me, she broke down in tears, asking when he'd be free and threatening to drop dead of a broken heart. Soon, he promised, he'd be free. Any day now. Maybe this month or next. He couldn't bear to tell her the truth—that unless they managed to win an appeal, he'd be there for many more years. They just had to sit in prison and wait for their futures.

Prison was another invisible city where they felt disappeared and largely forgotten. As in all societies, incarceration demographics in Greece tended to mirror the makeup of society's outcasts and neglected; many immigrants and refugees, now, filled Greek prison cells. Like Moria, this becomes another "bottleneck for people seeking a new home," as Thi had put it in her book *The Best We Could Do*, a holding pen for stalled lives and disintegrating myths. What few connections the young men had in Greece had been severed by their conviction. It was hard to keep in touch from inside, and their refugee friends were afraid to keep ties, they explained, lest such contact implicate them, somehow, in the fires.

As prisons go, Avlona wasn't the worst place they could be. It was home, in fact, to an internationally recognized education program that allowed them to take classes in a range of subjects, work toward high school and even college diplomas, and improve both their English and their Greek. But for what sort of life, in the end—and where?

In September 2021, just after the one-year anniversary of the Moria fire, I visited Sedique and her friends at the gallery in Mytilene. Earlier that week, a consortium of NGOs had organized an art exhibition commemorating the fire. Sedique and Fatimah showed me the canvases their team of artists had painted from that night: images full of blaze and shadow, people running, buildings burning, faces cast in postures of sorrow. One painting depicted a line of people silhouetted against an irradiated, yellow-orange sky. In the top corner of the painting, a flaming demon bellowed down toward the refugees, a burning tree in its claws.

"I think the devil here is a symbol of someone or something that has displaced people," Sedique reflected.

Seen this way, the fire wasn't just a fire, but a manifestation of the larger forces at play on the lives of refugees on Lesbos, and beyond. It brought to mind something the attorney Effie Doussi had said when I first met her: that Moria burning wasn't merely the story of a fire but "a chronicle of a disaster foretold."

Eventually I sent a picture of the devil painting to Ali and asked what he made of it.

"It looks like we are evil," he wrote.

I worried he thought that I was suggesting he was the devil in the image, or that I was accusing him of lying about his role in the fires, and I wrote him to explain that I hadn't meant to suggest as much.

"It's true we didn't start the fires," his reply read, "but if someone sees this painting and he doesn't know our story, he'll think we did it and that we are bad." Ali couldn't escape the accusations and the way he'd been portrayed at trial. He couldn't escape metabolizing, in some way, the story of his guilt.

After a long wait, the future arrived: the day the four eldest of the Moria 6 appealed their case. The defense team was ready. They had obtained translated copies of the original birth certificates from Afghanistan confirming that three of the four defendants were minors. They had new medical data showing the same. And they had commissioned a report to investigate the fire and compare its findings against the testimony of the eyewitnesses and the other official documents.

The report, created by a multimedia human rights firm called Forensic Architecture, was presented as a thorough video timeline of the night of the fire and its aftermath. It opens with the sound of crackling flames and a pan of the camp, burning—"reducing to ashes," as the narrator explains, "the epicenter of the European Union's carceral archipelago."

To complete this report, the Forensic Architecture team used metadata from hundreds of photos and videos taken on the night of the fire, mapping them on 3D imaging of the camp they'd created via drone footage, to track when and where the fires began and how they spread. It showed that the witness who had implicated the Moria 6 had indeed been lying when he said he saw them lighting fires in Zone 9 from his tent in Zone 12 late at night on September 8, for that zone hadn't even caught fire until the next morning. As the fire report had posited, it was the wind that had brought the fire to Zone 9, carrying embers from the center of the camp—what the Forensic Architecture report called "red snow"—on the air.

The genius of the Forensic Architecture report was that it rested on evidence provided by the refugees of Moria camp themselves—they had it right there on their phones. In aggregate, these scraps of memory completed the story of the fire, and of the Moria 6's innocence. I'd been looking all over, but the refugees had had the map all along.

And now it would be screened during the appeals trial for everyone to see.

It was a bluebird Monday in March 2023, and six cases were scheduled ahead of the Moria fire trial. I got to the courthouse early, waiting in the sun and watching an elderly gentleman in the building's second-story window spend many minutes wrestling with the Greek flag, trying to untangle it from its pole. The lawyers assembled in the courtyard: Effie, Natasha, Vicky, and others I'd interviewed over the years. They appeared visibly older since I'd first met them. I'm sure I did, too. Nearby, clusters of other journalists adjusted their cameras and flashed their credentials to the roving police. Across the street, a crew of hunched northern European volunteers—barred from the courthouse for having no official business there—smoked cigarettes and drank their coffees in front of a hand-scrawled sign: *Free the Moria 6! A Fair and Transparent Trial!*

A little after nine, a police van scuttled to a halt in front of the courthouse gates and a masked police officer flung open the doors, ordering the defendants to get out: *Pame, pame! Let's go, let's go!* Ali and Hassan emerged first, followed by the other two. I was moved to see that both pairs were holding hands—but then I realized that they had been cuffed together at the wrist. They walked inside and were seated in the back of the courtroom.

The first case was called to order, and then the second, and then the third. The day seemed to grow longer and longer, the horizon ever receding. Around three, the judges announced that unfortunately there'd be no time to hear the remaining cases. The Moria trial would be reset for Wednesday, two days hence. Effie respectfully pointed out that there was a national strike planned for Wednesday, in response to a massive train wreck in Greece the week earlier in which dozens of people had been killed and injured. The officials insisted the strike wouldn't affect the court.

Come Wednesday, the same judges announced that the case couldn't be heard because of the strike. It was reset for March 2024—an entire year later. And that was that. The young men were loaded back up into the van, taken back to their cells at the police station, and then eventually ushered onto the ferry, Athens-bound. The next time I spoke with Hassan, I told him how sorry I was that he'd have to keep waiting, and how unjust this timeline seemed to be.

"That's okay," he said. "Nothing to do," as in, *nothing to be done.* Maybe, he and Ali both told me, they'd get an earlier court date. Maybe. Their lawyers were working on it. In the meantime, they were back to waiting for the future. He'd do everything he could to get out of Greece, Hassan told me early on, because of everything that had befallen him there. "This place has really broken my heart."

Had the Forensic Architecture video been screened in court as planned, the judges would have heard that the original conviction had been "based on weak and contradictory evidence, suggest[ing] the inhumane management of the camp by Greece and the EU required a scapegoat for a disaster that was destined to happen." The Moria 6—Ali, Hassan, the others—were this very scapegoat. "The tragedy of Moria," read the ending lines of the video, "does not ultimately lie in its final act of burning, but in its very existence."

. . .

More tragedies still: in spring 2023 *The New York Times* published a video taken from the island of Lesbos that clearly showed men in Hellenic Coast Guard uniforms and balaclavas escorting a group of refugees onto a Coast Guard vessel and then abandoning them at sea. The Greek government said it would investigate the video. It was election season. "The hellhole of Moria . . . is no more," Prime Minister Mitsotakis told supporters during a campaign visit to Lesbos just weeks before the election. "It belongs to the past." He touted his administration's policies for bringing about a 90 percent drop in "illegal" migration since 2015. "We proved that the sea has borders, and that those borders can and must be protected," he said.

And then a rickety ship left Libya carrying some seven hundred people. It was bound for Italy but was blown into Greek waters. The captain and passengers repeatedly signaled distress. "Dozens of officials and coast guard crews monitored the ship," journalists for the *Times* would later write, "yet the Greek government treated the situation like a law enforcement operation, not a rescue." Because it was overloaded with panicked crowds and perhaps even because of a calamitous Coast Guard tow, the boat canted dramatically to the left, then to the right, and then tipped over. Passengers below deck were trapped; those above deck were hurled into the sea. Scattered amid the waves off the coast of Pylos, they flailed and gasped. Few knew how to swim. Some six hundred people drowned or were never found. In elections held soon after the disaster, Mitsotakis's party won in a landslide—despite these new deaths for lack of a timely rescue, despite the pushbacks, despite accusations against his administration of wiretapping political opponents, and of incompetence that led to the calamitous train crash that killed fifty-seven Greeks just a month before. Mitsotakis would stay on as prime minister. Meanwhile, a new rabidly far-right party, endorsed by the imprisoned leader of Golden Dawn, won 3 percent of the national vote. The near future had been written.

Throughout my reporting in Greece, I kept hearing a story that, because of the way people told it—like an incantation or a fable or a warning—reminded me of the story of the Indian woman in the Darién Gap. This story was about a pregnant woman from Afghanistan who, upon learning that her transfer from Lesbos to Germany was postponed a few months, doused herself with gasoline and lit a match. She'd had enough of this life of limbo; instantly her body was engulfed in flames. Against the odds, though, she and the baby survived the immolation. She was taken to the hospital, barely conscious. She was still drugged and covered in bandages when the police began interrogating her, and she was ultimately charged with arson in a Greek court.

I understood this story to be factually true and also a potent parable of the desperation of forced migration on the Greek islands, of the cruelty of the authorities, of the global criminalization of migrants—blamed for anything under the sun, including their own misery and despair, and made to pay for it. Another chronicle of a disaster foretold.

In the intractable context of forced migration here and throughout the world, where refugees are so often rendered as criminals and disappeared, fire can be regarded as both an inevitability and a matter of last resort. It was clear that the Moria 6 hadn't set the fires—there was simply no proof. But if the fire was indeed something more than mere accident? Would it be so surprising that someone might have decided to rewrite the Moria story by burning it all down?

On the surface, my family's story has nothing to do with Ali's or Hassan's, nothing to do with Sedique's, nothing much to do anymore, even, with Greece. And yet this is its own form of myth, for of course where our people came from helps determine who we are, and we cannot reckon with the injustices of contemporary migration without studying the migrations of the past—both the facts of these journeys and the way the accounts of them have been constructed in hindsight. For the way we tell stories isn't a mere matter of decency or morality; by influencing the way events are understood—a woman's self-immolation, a catastrophic shipwreck, an ancestor's journey across the sea many years ago—our stories determine the policies that are made and in turn whether people are welcomed in or deported home, jailed or set free—whether, even, they live or die. In this way our stories, and our fates, are all intertwined—like the trees.

What to do about the future? It seems we must excavate the stories we tell—looking not toward some idealized past, but to scrutinize who we have been as individuals and collectives, the mythologies that have guided us, and how we have so far lived. From there, we may be able to co-construct new, less ruinous storylines, new forms of belonging beyond borders. At the very least we might, like Robert Desnos, imagine into being stories that last long enough to matter.

The day I visited the gallery in Mytilene to see the fire paintings, Sedique had confided in me that she was particularly nervous because her parents' asylum appeal interview was scheduled for the next morning. They'd already been rejected twice; this was their final shot.

"We're just hoping," she said. "We're just hoping and praying for the best."

The fire paintings were stacked against the wall in the upstairs section of the gallery, where they'd been stored since the anniversary event. But the paintings they really wanted to show me, Sedique and Fatimah said, were downstairs, where canvases covered every square foot of wall space. In contrast to the upstairs stacks, most of these paintings were happy ones: smiling children, bucolic landscapes, scenes of levity, of fantasy, of delight.

"This one is the best one," Fatimah announced with zeal, leading me to a large canvas hung high on the north-facing wall. It was Sedique's painting. In it, a fair-skinned woman dressed in a billowing, fire-red ball gown was suspended over a glimmering sea, mid-leap. In the distance spread an open belt of green land. It looked like Greece, but in this painting there were no leaky rafts, no Coast Guard ships, no barbed wire, no ravenous flames—in the world Sedique painted, not even the laws of gravity seemed to apply.

I asked her what had moved her to paint it.

"I just liked it," she said. It was the future she was interested in, for by now she had spent more than enough time looking backward. She was tired of talking about the fires, of thinking about Moria and the Taliban and the boys in prison and her family's asylum case and all the bad things she'd survived. "Obsession with the past," Svetlana Boym had written, "might shortchange our future."

I loved Sedique's painting. It was a much more beautiful map than the one marred with borders, or the one I kept unfolding before her of

Moria before it burned, in the hope that she would help me untie the knots in the story I had been attempting to write. Her painting was a reclaimed narrative, too, of a young woman in flight—even, perhaps, a wishful oracle for the future.

"I liked it," she repeated, looking at the thing she'd made. "I just wanted to paint something beautiful."

Acknowledgments

Oh, the many people who made this book possible, and my life as I wrote it. Thank you to my excellent and loving editor, Becky Saletan, who saw this book both for what it was and, most important, for what it could be, and who helped me get it there with warmth, tenacity, and the sharpest of eyes. And to Julia Kardon, for taking a chance on this book, and on me. It's an honor to work with an agent committed to art and to justice. In the Sources section that follows, I express my gratitude to the books, writers, and thinkers who bolstered this book, but I want to say here that no book is written in isolation. This one, as does my entire writing life, owes everything to my life as a reader.

It also owes much to other writers who so generously became my readers and collaborators, even when this book was new and ill-formed—even before there were any words on the page. Thanks to Thi Bui, with whom I first traveled to Lesbos, and whose work and mind are a constant inspiration to me. Thanks also to my friend and teaching partner, Chris Feliciano Arnold, whose work as a writer, reporter, and educator has pushed my own practices. Jen Bowen Hicks, on behalf of editors from the Minnesota Prison Writing Workshop, commissioned an early essay that served as the portal into this book. The brilliant, big-hearted Robin MacArthur read through a very messy early manuscript draft and offered both much-needed enthusiasm and insight into how to give it shape; Ricardo Jaramillo provided his capacious mind and commitment to the fusion of beauty and meaning; the loving and rigorous Sierra Murdoch helped me articulate the book's central project and connect its many threads in the opening pages. Hillary Brenhouse read a draft of the book right before I first traveled to Greece to report on the Moria fire and, alchemist and seer that she is, helped me understand how it grafted to the larger questions of the book. Rebecca Solnit's friendship and championing have been a gift for more than a decade now, and I don't know how I got so lucky as to spend so much time in the presence of such a great mind and heart. Reese Kwon and Ingrid Rojas Contreras read early drafts and provided their trademark brilliant feedback, while also providing the consistent company, insight, love, and encouragement one needs to write a book and to make a life of words; every day, through their own work and lives, they reflect to me the writer that I want to be both on and off the page. (It's a beautiful thing that writing brought us together.) And perhaps no one helped mirror back to me this book's deepest purpose than Harriet Clark, whose insights are everywhere in these pages.

I found out I was pregnant while on a reporting trip to Greece. I completed a draft in the nausea that plagued me the entire pregnancy, and then worked through revisions from the very early days of postpartum, finishing right around my daughter's first birthday. What this means is that I owe a great deal to the people (including many of those named above) who took care of me in body and spirit and mind during those months, and to those who cared for my baby so that I could work. Thank you to Isa Gucciardi and Laura Chandler; to Larry Arrington, Alex Stickler, Alana Diamos, Ilka Fanni, and Meadow Evans for supporting our safe passage. Lenny Gucciardi and Connie Downing gave so much of their time to take care of our baby. My heroic mom visited frequently, always bringing relief and helping hands. We found Evelyn Easton Koehler on the internet, by chance, but she felt like a gift only the heavens could provide, as she took care of our tiny, fragile baby while I, also fragile, retreated into my backyard to write, to read, and sometimes just to weep. Then Kamela Dris swooped in during the final summer, bringing more brightness and care into our home. I am indebted to these caretakers.

Thanks to the brilliant Melissa Chou, who accompanied me to Greece on an epic trip in 2021; I couldn't have accomplished what I did there without her. Thanks also to my senior economic correspondent, Eric Skaar, for organizing a pandemic book club with Professor Thierry Warren, who in turn offered key insight into the Greek debt crisis and the geopolitics of southern Europe. Throughout the book's life span, Jude Dry offered long-distance friendship, love, and storytelling that have kept me laughing and afloat. Dani Fisher, one of my oldest friends, has done so from nearby. Meanwhile, Kate Bryan Brown and Lindsay Whalen kept me company via video message in the early days of parenting, and to this day; from time zones away, they bolster me with strategy and with laughter. And there is no one who takes care of me like Hannah Epstein—who listens to every gripe and worry and dream and joke and idea and opinion, no matter how tired or busy or bored she may be.

This project is also indebted to the time of many advocates and residents of the Aegean Islands. I am particularly appreciative of the team at Legal Centre Lesvos for their patience with my questions. Early conversations with Chloe Haralambous led me down some critical research rabbit holes; her intellect, expansive knowledge, and generosity were invaluable to this book's earliest stages. Thank you, too, to Sappho for hosting (and interpreting) my visits to Klio. And thank you to both

Thanasis Voulgarakis and Noori Alam for navigation and interpretation support in Greece, and for their friendship. Thanks, too, to my former students Asma Maqsoodi and Mohammad Aseel for phone interpretation (you two make me very proud). Above all, thanks to those who allowed me to share their stories within these pages.

I am grateful to the Borchard Foundation Center on Literary Arts, the Pulitzer Center on Crisis Reporting, the Society of Environmental Journalists, and the de Groot Foundation's Lando Award for providing critical funding that made it possible to carry out ambitious research, travel, and writing. A few editors commissioned pieces related to migration and justice in Greece, which helped me sort through the ideas and politics that undergird this book. Thank you to Ian Gordon at *Mother Jones*, Rachel Dry at *The New York Times*, and Clare Longrigg at *The Guardian*, as well as Vauhini Vara and Julie Just. I am grateful to Alex Brock, who vigorously checked my facts, assumptions, and errors throughout the text (all hail fact-checkers!). And Lydia Emmanouilidou, with whom I cowrote a piece for the *Times*, buoyed me with energy, clarity, and expertise at a time when I needed it; she also provided invaluable comments on a late draft of this book.

I am so appreciative of Jonathan Blitzer, Thi Bui, Aminatta Forna, Adam Hochschild, Leslie Jamison, Ingrid Rojas Contreras, and Rebecca Solnit for their early words of support and for reading these pages when so many other books and aspects of life demand their attention. This book wouldn't exist without my family, both those alive and those who have passed, and their abundant stories and myths. Thank you for these, for passing along the joys and the sorrows, and for making me who I am. A particular thanks to Penny Boling, Jesse Markham, Jr., Betsy McLean, and my dad, to whom this book is dedicated.

And thank you to Ben, my poet, my love, who believed in *A Map of*

Future Ruins, and knew what I needed to do in order to start it, long before I did. He always knows. He read page upon page, listened to so many of my stories, worries, anxieties, and hopes, and cared so lovingly for our daughter while I went away—to Greece, to hotels here and there to work, to the backyard—so this book could be. And thank you to sweet Clio, our muse of history, eyes like oracles: our bright and growing future.

Sources

I spent roughly four years intensively reporting, researching, and writing *A Map of Future Ruins*, though in retrospect, this book is the product of an entire career—and life—spent thinking about borders and belonging.

The vast majority of the on-the-ground reporting for this book was conducted in Greece between 2019 and 2023—sometimes in the course of magazine assignments and sometimes explicitly for the book. I interviewed countless people and spent many, many hours with former residents of Moria and other refugees in Greece, as well as attorneys, advocates, NGO workers, UN officials, Greek citizens (many from the Aegean Islands), Greek politicians, and other authorities.

Some of my magazine writing reappears in this book, in slightly or significantly altered form. The material on pushbacks was first published in my 2022 story "The Pushback" for *Mother Jones*, and some of the material on the Moria fire first appeared in my 2022 *Guardian* piece, "'A Disaster Waiting to Happen': Who Is Really to Blame for the Destruction of Moria Refugee Camp?" Reporting for my 2022 *New York Times* story, coauthored with journalist Lydia Emmanouilidou, "How Free Is the Press in the Birthplace of Democracy?" provided additional insight into the issues discussed in this book, as did another piece I wrote for the *Times* in 2021, "The Unnecessary Cruelty of America's Immigration System." I've included excerpts from earlier work in these pages, too: my 2018 *Harper's Magazine* article "If These Walls Could Talk," a 2018 article for *The New Republic* titled "'This Route Doesn't Exist on the Map,'" and a 2020 piece from the *Virginia Quarterly Review* on vicarious trauma, "No End in Sight." I also refer to reporting on trees that I conducted for a *Mother Jones* assignment, "Can We Move Our Forests in Time to Save Them?"

Naturally, the memoir and travelogue sections of this book were reported as experienced: firsthand. Reporting on my ancestry required archival research.

I relied heavily on the digitized records of Ellis Island, which are a true treasure trove of facts as well as fodder for wistful imagining about what once was and what might have been. I also relied on the participation and assistance of members of my beloved family, whom I've thanked by name above.

The more journalistic aspects of the book were assembled through a combination of firsthand reporting and reconstruction. Any event for which I was present has been reported accordingly but also meticulously fact-checked. For events for which I was not present, I have relied on the accounts of others—from history texts to personal memories to documentary evidence—to recreate scenes and stories, comparing as many sources as I could find in order to arrive as close as possible to the truth of what happened. Wherever I found discrepancies in the accounts, or holes in my sources, I have noted that, in the spirit of transparency.

The facts included in this book have all been verified by an independent fact-checker; where it was impossible to do so, I have made clear in the text that the recollections were those of a single individual or group. In the case of the Moria trial, for instance, the prosecutors representing the Greek government and the local and national fire departments repeatedly refused to provide any evidence or facts on the case. I thus had to rely exclusively on the accounts of the accused and the arguments and evidence presented by the defense in order to reconstruct the trial, as I make clear in the narrative. Other accounts in the book—such as the memories of a shipwreck, for instance, or of running from the fire—are difficult, if not impossible, to fully verify. In such cases I checked whatever I could and then took the account at face value, narrating it as a story told to me. I do so with the conviction that it is important to believe the testimonies of people on the move, and also with the understanding that memory is fallible. I trust that readers can hold both of these truths at once.

Reporting on the lives of the Moria 6 proved especially challenging, given the fact that they were locked up and I wasn't permitted to visit them in person. Through the exchange of written messages and the occasional phone call (which I translated thanks to the help of several excellent translators) I was able to reconstruct some of their stories in this book. Where possible, I cross-referenced their memories with those of their families or friends.

Because I don't live in Greece, I relied heavily on Greek journalism and journalists as I followed the events there from afar—coverage, in particular, in NPR, *The Guardian*, *Solomon*, Reporters United, *eKathimerini*, *Greek Reporter*, and *Der Spiegel* and by Al Jazeera and *Inside Story*. I owe deep gratitude to the journalists reporting for these and other outlets, and to the Greek journalists most of all. Many of them are working in conditions increasingly hostile to journalism and to truth-telling, and they strive to shine the light all the same.

What follows is an extensive bibliography of texts that influenced this book. Some of the sources listed helped me to secure facts or to clarify important sociopolitical dynamics. Others provided deep touchstones as I worked to expand my knowledge, understanding, and perspectives on central issues.

With regard to the latter category: Roderick Beaton's tremendous *Greece: Biography of a Modern Nation* provided an invaluable perspective on Greek history and helped me fill the many gaps in my historical knowledge. Yanis Varoufakis's *Adults in the Room: My Battle with Europe's Deep Establishment* did even more to complete the picture of the Greek debt crisis and the very long shadow it casts on the country's economy and politics. The fiction of Christos Ikonomou, which I first read on the beach in Andros, moved me deeply, and offered human insight into the costs and casualties of the debt crisis in the way that only fiction can. William Broad's *The Oracle* is a stunning book on the Oracle at Delphi—its history, mythologies, fandom, and science, and the remarkable quest of a geologist and an archaeologist to plumb its depths and meaning. Mark Monmonier's *How to Lie with Maps* helped me to more deeply understand the power and contradiction of cartography and its role in nation-building, deception, and power. Vangelis Calotychos's *Modern Greece: A Cultural Poetics* offered vital insight into the construction of Greek identity by outsiders and insiders alike, and the tension between the two. Wendy Brown's *Walled States, Waning Sovereignty* provided a key comparative framework for our age of border walls, and offered sharp insight and explanation about its causes. (These books also helped me through a long illness in 2020, and helped to create intellectual pathways toward a book that felt, at the time, like both an imperative and an impossibility.)

No work was as profoundly instrumental to me as Svetlana Boym's *The Future of Nostalgia* (recommended to me onstage by the great Aleksandar Hemon just when I was mustering the courage to begin this book). Maggie Nelson offers the notion of what she calls a "ghost book," "a book that secretly—or not so secretly, as the case may be—stands behind my book, not just as its muse, but often as its literal stylistic and/or structural model." *The Future of Nostalgia* is my ghost book. The ideas in Boym's book endowed my own ideas, and my own book, with rigor and with spirit—and greater life.

"AIA Condemns Executive Order Mandating Design Preference for Federal Architecture." American Institute of Architects, December 21, 2020. https://www.aia.org/press-releases/6359953-aia-condemns-executive-order-mandating-des.

"Aliens Removed or Returned: Fiscal Years 1892 to 2019" (table). U.S. Department of Homeland Security. https://www.dhs.gov/immigration-statistics/yearbook/2019/table39.

"Alternatives to ICE Detention for Non-Citizens of the United States." LIRS (Lutheran Immigration and Refugee Service), January 27, 2021. https://www.lirs.org/alternatives-ice-detention-united-states/.

Amenyah, Odelia, and Grace Kovar. "Ethnic Hostility Was Entrenched in Omaha: The Anti-Greek Riots of 1909." *Omaha World-Herald*, December 18, 2022. https://omaha.com/ethnic-hostility-was-entrenched-in-omaha-the-anti-greek-riots-of-1909/article_c2710820-7ce7-11ed-a889-43a944e27f66.html.

Appiah, Kwame Anthony. "There Is No Such Thing as Western Civilisation." *The Guardian*, November 9, 2016. https://www.theguardian.com/world/2016/nov/09/western-civilisation-appiah-reith-lecture.

Arimont, Pascal. "Situation in the Moria Refugee Camp on Lesvos: Priority Question for Written Answer P-003742/2019 to the Commission, Rule 138." Parliamentary Question P-003742/2019, European Parliament, August 11, 2019. https://www.europarl.europa.eu/doceo/document/P-9-2019-003742_EN.html.

Associated Press. "More Than 300 Refugees Planned for Rutland." WCAX, Rutland, Vermont, May 20, 2022. https://www.wcax.com/2022/05/20/more-than-300-refugees-planned-rutland/.

Baker, Camille. "From the Mediterranean to Mexico, Capt. Pia Klemp Believes Rescuing Refugees Is Worth Facing Prison Time." *The Intercept*, July 10, 2019. https://theintercept.com/2019/07/10/mediterranean-migrant-rescue-pia-klemp/.

Baker, Patrick, Johannes Helmrath, and Craig Kallendorf. *Beyond Reception: Renaissance Humanism and the Transformation of Classical Antiquity*. Berlin and Boston: De Gruyter, 2019.

Bauer, Shane. "The True History of America's Private Prison Industry." *Time*, September 25, 2018. https://time.com/5405158/the-true-history-of-americas-private-prison-industry/.

Bausells, Marta, and Maeve Shearlaw. "Poets Speak Out for Refugees: 'No One Leaves Home, Unless Home Is the Mouth of a Shark.'" *The Guardian*, September 16, 2015. https://www.theguardian.com/books/2015/sep/16/poets-speak-out-for-refugees-.

Beaton, Roderick. *Greece: Biography of a Modern Nation*. Chicago: University of Chicago Press, 2019.

Blair, Elizabeth. "'Ugly,' 'Discordant': New Executive Order Takes Aim at Modern Architecture." NPR, December 21, 2020. https://www.npr.org/2020/02/13/805256707/just-plain-ugly-proposed-executive-order-takes-aim-at-modern-architecture.

Bond, Kate, and Gordon Welters. "Help to Vulnerable on Lesvos Wins Efi Latsoudi 2016 Nansen Award." UNHCR, The UN Refugee Agency/USA, September 6, 2016. https://www.unhcr.org/us/news/stories/help-vulnerable-lesvos-wins-efi-latsoudi-2016-nansen-award.

Bowen, Scott, and Muin J. Khoury. "Consumer Genetic Testing Is Booming: But What Are the Benefits and Harms to Individuals and Populations?" *Genomics and Precision Health* (blog), Centers for Disease Control and Prevention, June 12, 2018. https://blogs.cdc.gov/genomics/2018/06/12/consumer-genetic-testing/.

Boym, Svetlana. *The Future of Nostalgia*. New York: Basic Books, 2002.

———. "A Soviet Drop-Out's Journey to Freedom." *Tablet*, July 3, 2014. https://www.tabletmag.com/sections/arts-letters/articles/camp-tale.

Broad, William J. *The Oracle: Ancient Delphi and the Science Behind Its Lost Secrets*. New York: Penguin Books, 2007.

Brown, Wendy. *Walled States, Waning Sovereignty*. Cambridge, MA: MIT Press, 2014.

Calotychos, Vangelis. *Modern Greece: A Cultural Poetics*. Oxford: Berg, 2004.

Campbell, Joseph. *The Hero with a Thousand Faces*. London: HarperCollins UK, 1988.

"Cash-Strapped Greece Struggles Against Overwhelming Tide of Refugees." *PBS News Weekend*, November 1, 2015. https://www.pbs.org/newshour/show/greece-refugees.

"Common European Asylum System." European Commission, Migration and Home Affairs. https://home-affairs.ec.europa.eu/policies/migration-and-asylum/common-european-asylum-system_en.

Condit, Celeste M., Nneka Ofulue, and Kristine M. Sheedy. "Determinism and Mass-Media Portrayals of Genetics." *American Journal of Human Genetics* 62, no. 4 (April 1998): 979–84. https://doi.org/10.1086/301784.

"The Cost of Immigration Enforcement and Border Security." American Immigration Council, January 2021. https://www.americanimmigrationcouncil.org/sites/default/files/research/the_cost_of_immigration_enforcement_and_border_security.pdf.

Davis, Ben. "The New White Nationalism's Sloppy Use of Art History, Decoded." *Artnet News*, March 7, 2017. https://news.artnet.com/art-world/identity-evropa-posters-art-symbolism-881747.

Deeb, Bashar, et al. "Unmasking Europe's Shadow Armies." Lighthouse Reports, October 6, 2021. https://www.lighthousereports.com/investigation/unmasking-europes-shadow-armies/.

Digidiki, Vasileia, and Jacqueline Bhabha. "Greece's Proposed 'Floating Wall' Shows the Failure of EU Migration Policies." *The Guardian*, February 7, 2020. https://www.theguardian.com/commentisfree/2020/feb/07/greece-floating-wall-eu-refugees-migrant-policy.

Eagly, Ingrid, and Steven Shafer. "Access to Counsel in Immigration Court." American Immigration Council Special Report, September 2016. https://www.americanimmigrationcouncil.org/sites/default/files/research/access_to_counsel_in_immigration_court.pdf.

"1891: Immigration Inspection Expands." U.S. Customs and Border Protection. https://www.cbp.gov/about/history/1891-imigration-inspection-expands.

Eliot, T. S. *The Waste Land*. Edited by Michael North. New York: W. W. Norton, 2001.

Emmanouilidou, Lydia. "Migrants Displaced by Fire at Moria Camp on Lesbos: 'Nobody's Life Is Safe Here.'" *The World*, September 14, 2020. https://theworld.org/stories/2020-09-14/migrants-displaced-fire-moria-camp-lesbos-nobody-s-life-safe-here.

——. "Thousands of Refugees Sleep in Streets After Fire Destroys Greece's Moria Camp." *The World*, September 11, 2020. https://theworld.org/stories/2020-09-11/thousands-refugees-sleep-streets-after-fire-destroys-greeces-moria-camp.

Fallon, Katy. "Heavily Criticised Trial of Activists Adjourned in Greece." Al Jazeera, November 18, 2021. https://www.aljazeera.com/news/2021/11/18/dozens-of-activists-face-trial-for-refugee-work-in-greece.

——, and Stavros Malichudis. "A Fire in Tent 959." *Solomon*, May 3, 2021. https://wearesolomon.com/mag/focus-area/migration/a-fire-in-tent-959/.

Fermor, Patrick Leigh. *Roumeli: Travels in Northern Greece*. London: Hachette UK, 2010.

"Fire in Moria Refugee Camp." Forensic Architecture, March 6, 2023. https://forensic-architecture.org/investigation/fire-in-moria-refugee-camp.

"Free the Moria 6: A Statement from the Defence Lawyers on the Unfair Trial of Four of Those Accused of the Moria Fires." Legal Centre Lesvos, June 25, 2021. http://legalcentrelesvos.org/2021/06/25/δηλωση-των-συνηγορων-υπερασπισησ-των/.

Ghosh, Smita. "How Migrant Detention Became American Policy." *The Washington Post*, July 19, 2019. https://www.washingtonpost.com/outlook/2019/07/19/how-migrant-detention-became-american-policy/.

Giles, Matt. "An Interview with MacArthur 'Genius' Jason De León." *Longreads*, October 18, 2017. https://longreads.com/2017/10/18/an-interview-with-macarthur-genius-jason-de-leon/.

"Gods in Color: Polychromy in Antiquity." Digitorial for exhibition, January 30, 2020–September 26, 2021, Liebieghaus, Frankfurt. https://buntegoetter.liebieghaus.de/en/.

Goodyer, Jason. "Cave Paintings Reveal Ancient Europeans' Knowledge of the Stars." *BBC Science Focus Magazine*, January 19, 2019. https://www.sciencefocus.com/planet-earth/cave-paintings-reveal-ancient-europeans-knowledge-of-the-stars/.

"Greece." UNHCR, The UN Refugee Agency, September 2020. https://www.unhcr.org/countries/greece.

"Greece: Four Afghan Migrants Jailed over Moria Camp Fire." Al Jazeera, June 13, 2021. https://www.aljazeera.com/news/2021/6/13/afghans-jailed-in-greece-over-moria-migrant-camp-blaze.

"Greece: Migrant Rescue Trial to Begin." Human Rights Watch, December 22, 2022. https://www.hrw.org/news/2022/12/22/greece-migrant-rescue-trial-begin.

"Greece: Refugee 'Hotspots' Unsafe, Unsanitary." Human Rights Watch, May 19, 2016. https://www.hrw.org/news/2016/05/19/greece-refugee-hotspots-unsafe-unsanitary.

Griffin, Susan. "To Love the Marigold: Hope & Imagination" (from *The Impossible Will Take a Little While: A Citizen's Guide to Hope in a Time of Fear*, edited by Paul Loeb). *Z*, January 27, 2005. https://znetwork.org/znetarticle/to-love-the-marigold-hope-and-imagination-by-susan-griffin/.

Gucciardi, Ben. "On the Shoreline." *Five Points* 21, no. 2.

———. "Prayer for the Instant City." *Indiana Review* 40, no. 2 (Winter 2018).

"Guiding Principles for Federal Architecture." U.S. General Services Administration. https://www.gsa.gov/real-estate/design-and-construction/design-excellence-program/guiding-principles.

Halley, Catherine. "September 1922: The Great Fire of Smyrna." *JSTOR Daily*, September 22, 2022. https://daily.jstor.org/september-1922-the-great-fire-of-smyrna/.

Hirschon, Renée, ed. *Crossing the Aegean: An Appraisal of the 1923 Compulsory Population Exchange between Greece and Turkey*. New York and Oxford: Berghahn Books, 2008.

Ikonomou, Christos. *Good Will Come from the Sea*. Translated by Karen Emmerich. Brooklyn, NY: Archipelago Books, 2019.

———. *Something Will Happen, You'll See*. Translated by Karen Emmerich. Brooklyn, NY: Archipelago Books, 2016.

"Immigrants and the Economy." American Civil Liberties Union, March 12, 2002. https://www.aclu.org/other/immigrants-and-economy.

"Immigration and Nationality Act of 1965 [October 3, 1965]." United States House of Representatives: History, Art & Archives." https://history.house.gov/Historical-Highlights/1951-2000/Immigration-and-Nationality-Act-of-1965/.

"Italy: Sea-Watch 3's Captain Must Not Be Prosecuted for Saving Lives." Amnesty International, July 2, 2019. https://www.amnesty.org/en/latest/news/2019/07/sea-watch-3-captain-must-not-be-prosecuted-for-saving-lives-2/.

"Justice for the Moria 6." Legal Centre Lesvos, March 9, 2021. http://legalcentrelesvos.org/2021/03/09/justice-for-the-moria-6/.

Kasimis, Charalambos, and Chryssa Kassimi. "Greece: A History of Migration." Migration Policy Institute, June 1, 2004. https://www.migrationpolicy.org/article/greece-history-migration.

Kassie, Emily. "How Trump Inherited His Expanding Detention System." The Marshall Project, February 12, 2019. https://www.themarshallproject.org/2019/02/12/how-trump-inherited-his-expanding-detention-system.

Keck, Nina. "He Was the Mayor Who Brought Refugees to Rutland. His Regret? Not Bringing More." *Vermont Public*, September 22, 2019. https://www.vermontpublic.org/vpr-news/2019-09-22/he-was-the-mayor-who-brought-refugees-to-rutland-his-regret-not-bringing-more.

Konstantinidis, Alkis. "Greece Opens New Migrant Holding Camp on Island amid Tougher Policy." Reuters, September 18, 2021. https://www.reuters.com/world/europe/greece-opens-new-migrant-holding-camp-island-amid-tougher-policy-2021-09-18/.

"'Lethal Disregard': Search and Rescue and the Protection of Migrants in the Central Mediterranean Sea." United Nations, Human Rights, Office of the High Commissioner, May 2021. https://www.ohchr.org/sites/default/files/Documents/Issues/Migration/OHCHR-thematic-report-SAR-protection-at-sea.pdf.

Malichudis, Stavros. "I Am the Journalist Being Watched by the Greek Secret Service." *Solomon*, November 16, 2021. https://wearesolomon.com/mag/our-news/i-am-the-journalist-being-watched-by-the-greek-secret-service/.

———. "Moria's 'Missing' Migrants." *Solomon*, February 8, 2023. https://wearesolomon.com/mag/focus-area/migration/morias-missing-migrants/.

——. "Ukraine War: The 'Real' Refugees and the Lies of the Greek Government." *Solomon*, March 22, 2022. https://wearesolomon.com/mag/focus-area/migration/ukraine-war-the-real-refugees-and-the-lies-of-the-greek-government/.

Marshall, Alex. "After 220 Years, the Fate of the Parthenon Marbles Rests in Secret Talks." *The New York Times*, January 17, 2023. https://www.nytimes.com/2023/01/17/arts/design/parthenon-sculptures-elgin-marbles-negotiations.html.

"Massive Protests by Islanders Are Challenging the Government's Narrative on New Prison Structures in the Aegean." RSA (Refugee Support Aegean), January 28, 2022. https://rsaegean.org/en/new-prison-structures-in-the-aegean/.

McKernan, Beth. "Alan Kurdi's Father Condemns Politicians for Failing to Act: 'People Are Still Dying and Nobody Is Doing Anything About It.'" *The Independent*, September 1, 2016. https://www.independent.co.uk/news/world/middle-east/alan-kurdi-anniversary-abdullah-syria-war-kobani-aylan-a7220481.html.

Mendelsohn, Daniel. "Deep Frieze." *The New Yorker*, April 7, 2014. https://www.newyorker.com/magazine/2014/04/14/deep-frieze.

——. *Three Rings: A Tale of Exile, Narrative, and Fate*. Charlottesville, VA: University of Virginia Press, 2020.

Michener, Kirsten. "Stress and Burnout Found among Nation's Immigration Judges." University of California San Francisco, June 25, 2009. https://www.ucsf.edu/news/2009/06/96756/stress-and-burnout-found-among-nations-immigration-judges.

"Milestones: 1921–1936: The Immigration Act of 1924 (The Johnson-Reed Act)." Office of the Historian, U.S. Department of State. https://history.state.gov/milestones/1921-1936/immigration-act.

Monmonier, Mark. *How to Lie with Maps*. Chicago: University of Chicago Press, 1996.

"Museum History." Acropolis Museum, Athens. https://www.theacropolismuseum.gr/en/museum-history.

Nail, Thomas. *Theory of the Border*. New York: Oxford University Press, 2016.

Office of Immigration Statistics. *2019 Yearbook of Immigration Statistics*. U.S. Department of Homeland Security, September 2020. https://www.dhs.gov/sites/default/files/publications/immigration-statistics/yearbook/2019/yearbook_immigration_statistics_2019.pdf.

Painter, Nell Irvin. *The History of White People*. New York: W. W. Norton, 2011.

Pantelia, Anna (@Anna_Pantelia). "This is the hero." Twitter, October 10, 2022, 3:35 p.m. https://twitter.com/Anna_Pantelia/status/1579556226492690432.

Papaioannou, Eva, Eva Petraki, and Betty Siafaka. "'We Can Only Help Our Patients to Survive' New Camp on Samos." Médecins Sans Frontières, September 17, 2021. https://www.msf.org/we-can-only-help-refugees-survive-new-camp-greek-island.

Pappas, Mitcho S. "The Greek Immigrant in the United States since 1910" (master's thesis, Montana State University, 1950). ScholarWorks, University of Montana. https://scholarworks.umt.edu/etd/5342.

The Passenger: Greece. London: Europa Editions UK, 2020.

Peri, Giovanni, and Reem Zaiour. "Citizenship for Undocumented Immigrants Would Boost U.S. Economic Growth." Center for American Progress, June 14, 2021. https://www.americanprogress.org/article/citizenship-undocumented-immigrants-boost-u-s-economic-growth/.

Petrarca, Francesco. *Selected Letters*, vol. 1. Translated by Elaine Fantham. Cambridge, MA: Harvard University Press, I Tatti Renaissance Library, 2017.

"Prime Minister Kyriakos Mitsotakis' Address to the Joint Session of the U.S. Congress." Office of the Prime Minister of the Hellenic Republic, May 17, 2022. https://www.primeminister.gr/en/2022/05/17/29339.

Procopio, Michael. "Horta Culture." KQED, San Francisco, July 26, 2013. https://www.kqed.org/bayareabites/66329/horta-culture.

Rael, Ronald. *Borderwall as Architecture: A Manifesto for the U.S.-Mexico Boundary*. Berkeley: University of California Press, 2017.

"Refugee Act of 1980." National Archives Foundation. https://www.archivesfoundation.org/documents/refugee-act-1980/.

"Refugee Timeline: Immigration and Naturalization Service Refugee Law and Policy Timeline, 1891–2003." U.S. Citizenship and Immigration Services, February 7, 2023. https://www.uscis.gov/about-us/our-history/history-office-and-library/featured-stories-from-the-uscis-history-office-and-library/refugee-timeline.

"Remarks by President Trump on the Illegal Immigration Crisis and Border Security." The White House, November 1, 2018. https://trumpwhitehouse.archives.gov/briefings-statements/remarks-president-trump-illegal-immigration-crisis-border-security/.

Reuters. "Greek Grandmother, Fisherman, Among Nobel Peace Nominees." Voice of America, February 1, 2016. https://www.voanews.com/a/greek-grandmother-fisherman-among-nobel-peace-nominees/3172813.html.

Ross, Edward Alsworth. *The Old World in the New: The Significance of Past and Present Immigration to the American People*. New York: Century, 1914.

Ross, John F. *The Promise of the Grand Canyon: John Wesley Powell's Perilous Journey and His Vision for the American West*. New York: Viking, 2018.

Scanlan, Chip. "The Nut Graf Tells the Reader What the Writer Is Up To." *Poynter*, May 19, 2003. https://www.poynter.org/archive/2003/the-nut-graf-part-i/.

"A Short History of Immigration Detention." Freedom for Immigrants. https://www.freedomforimmigrants.org/detention-timeline.

Smith, Colin. "Cyprus Divided: 40 Years On, a Family Recalls How the Island Was Torn Apart." *The Guardian*, July 6, 2014. https://www.theguardian.com/world/2014/jul/06/turkish-invasion-divided-cyprus-40-years-on-eyewitness-greek-cypriot-family.

Smith, Helena. "Bodies of 11 Refugees, Most of Them Infants, Recovered off Greece." *The Guardian*, November 1, 2015. https://www.theguardian.com/world/2015/nov/01/bodies-of-11-refugees-most-of-them-infants-recovered-off-greece.

———. "Greece Sets Out Emergency Plans to Tackle Surge of Migrant Arrivals." *The Guardian*, September 2, 2019. https://www.theguardian.com/world/2019/sep/02/greece-sets-out-emergency-plans-to-tackle-surge-of-migrant-arrivals.

———. "Shocking Images of Drowned Syrian Boy Show Tragic Plight of Refugees." *The Guardian*, September 2, 2015. https://www.theguardian.com/world/2015/sep/02/shocking-image-of-drowned-syrian-boy-shows-tragic-plight-of-refugees.

———. "'We Left Fearing for Our Lives': Doctors Set Upon by Mob in Lesbos." *The Guardian*, March 4, 2020. https://www.theguardian.com/world/2020/mar/04/we-left-fearing-for-our-lives-doctors-set-upon-by-mob-in-lesbos.

———. "Woman Who Set Herself on Fire in Lesbos Refugee Camp Charged with Arson." *The Guardian*, February 26, 2021. https://www.theguardian.com/world/2021/feb/26/woman-who-set-herself-on-fire-in-lesbos-refugee-camp-may-face-arson-charges.

Ssengendo, James. "Acropolis Receives Record 16,000 Visitors Daily." *Greek Reporter*, August 9, 2022. https://greekreporter.com/2022/08/09/acropolis-record-visitors-daily/.

"Statement for the Record: 'The Expansion and Troubling Use of ICE Detention.'" National Immigration Forum, September 25, 2019. https://immigrationforum.org/article/statement-for-the-record-the-expansion-and-troubling-use-of-ice-detention/.

"Statement from President Carter Commemorating the Anniversary of the Refugee Act of 1980." The Carter Center, March 17, 2021. https://www.cartercenter.org/news/pr/2021/president-carter-statement-031821.html.

"Statement on Preliminary Observations and Recommendations Following Official Visit to Greece." UN Special Rapporteur on Human Rights Defenders, June 22, 2022. https://srdefenders.org/statement-on-preliminary-observations-and-recommendations-following-official-visit-to-greece/.

"States Parties, Including Reservations and Declarations, to the 1951 Refugee Convention." UNHCR, The UN Refugee Agency. https://www.unhcr.org/media/38230.

Statista Research Department. "Deaths of Migrants in the Mediterranean Sea 2014–2022." Statista, February 10, 2023. https://www.statista.com/statistics/1082077/deaths-of-migrants-in-the-mediterranean-sea/.

Stevis-Gridneff, Matina, and Karam Shoumali. "Everyone Knew the Migrant Ship Was Doomed. No One Helped." *The New York Times*, July 3, 2023. https://www.nytimes.com/2023/07/01/world/europe/greece-migrant-ship.html.

Stevis-Gridneff, Matina, et al. "Greece Says It Doesn't Ditch Migrants at Sea. It Was Caught in the Act." *The New York Times*, May 19, 2023. https://www.nytimes.com/2023/05/19/world/europe/greece-migrants-abandoned.html.

Talbot, Margaret. "The Myth of Whiteness in Classical Sculpture." *The New Yorker*, October 22, 2018. https://www.newyorker.com/magazine/2018/10/29/the-myth-of-whiteness-in-classical-sculpture.

Taylor, Harry. "Greece Extends Border Wall to Deter Afghans Trying to Reach Europe." *The Guardian*, August 21, 2021. https://www.theguardian.com/world/2021/aug/21/greece-extends-border-wall-deter-afghans-trying-reach-europe.

Ther, Philipp. *The Outsiders: Refugees in Europe since 1492*. Princeton, NJ: Princeton University Press, 2021.

Tondo, Lorenzo. "'They Are Our Salvation': The Sicilian Town Revived by Refugees." *The Guardian*, March 19, 2018. https://www.theguardian.com/world/2018/mar/19/sutera-italy-the-sicilian-town-revived-by-refugees.

Trilling, Daniel. "Golden Dawn: The Rise and Fall of Greece's Neo-Nazis." *The Guardian*, March 3, 2020. https://www.theguardian.com/news/2020/mar/03/golden-dawn-the-rise-and-fall-of-greece-neo-nazi-trial.

"2019: A Deadly Year for Migrants Crossing the Americas." *UN News*, January 28, 2020. https://news.un.org/en/story/2020/01/1056202.

Varoufakis, Yanis. *Adults in the Room: My Battle with Europe's Deep Establishment*. New York: Vintage, 2018.

Walia, Harsha. *Border and Rule: Global Migration, Capitalism, and the Rise of Racist Nationalism*. Chicago: Haymarket Books, 2021.

"War (Πόλεμος)." *Organically Greek* (blog), February 21, 2010. http://organicallycooked.blogspot.com/2010/02/war.html.

Washington, John. *The Dispossessed: A Story of Asylum at the US-Mexico Border and Beyond*. New York: Verso, 2020.

Watkins, William H. "Race and Morality: Shaping the Myth." In *Conflict, Contradiction and Contrarian Elements in Moral Development and Education*, edited by Larry Nucci. London: Routledge, 2016.

"What Is the EU-Turkey Deal?" International Rescue Committee, March 18, 2022, updated March 16, 2023. https://www.rescue.org/eu/article/what-eu-turkey-deal.